A Purple Sky

Other books by Rob Matchett

Native Woodnotes Wild: 101 Sonnets
Among the Blueberries
Apocalypta: A Novel From the Future
People of the Sky
Shake-speare's Oedipus
A Fish Fell From the Sky
Pedro the Enigma

FILM SCRIPTS
People of the Sky
A Fish Fell From the Sky
Shake-speare: Oxford's Lost Manuscripts
Ghostwitch

UP-COMING TITLES
Fresh Lava: Early Poems

FILM SCRIPT
Dead Sea: I Am the Word

A Purple Sky

ROB MATCHETT

Book design by Brady Type

National Library of Canada Cataloguing in Publication
A purple sky : an epic poem / by Rob Matchett.
ISBN 978-0-9917233-8-6 (print)
ISBN 9780-1-928026-02-0 (ebook)
I. Title.
PS8576.A7996P74 2003   C811'.54   C2003-900144-X
PR9199.3.M3935P74 2003

Prologue

I, Zephyrus, must tell a tale,
One that shears of a wicked gale,
Bestirring new times awaken
A goddess long since forsaken…
Recalled from my desolate space,
To make known our prescient place,
A bequest of sorts for my role,
A true telling upon my soul –
If not human at least of kin,
For dear Raven, who died herein…
She was of iridescent light
Radiating ever so bright,
Given in some measure of fate –
A woman to whom we relate
So prodigious in stature,
Renowned as Mother Nature –
Did the fruit of knowledge partake
Such as Aphrodite of the lake…
From her love rivers did wend
To the ocean beyond lands end,
As she inspired in spite of blame,
The beauty of her sacred flame…

One

Swoop, Zephyrus, curious mimes,
Burn, with these my spurious rhymes,
Rain, snuff fire of furious times,
Blow, fair wind, of glorious climes…
Yet no way out from time that reaps
Lifelines worked, or how well it suits
Loves skyward kiss, which singing leaps
With the force of a thousand flutes...
And so murmurs water sounds
Put to dreams with sleepy sigh –
To this day her myth abounds,
Tendered to a purple sky…
       Heed now what must ensue –
       Ride the wind in my parvenu...

✲

Among the wild lands of the north,
Where summer and winter turn forth,
And deep blue lakes of cool water,
There lived a native daughter…

With long black hair like shining silk,
Brown eyes and skin like cocoa milk,
Lithe and blithe who yet tough and bold,
Disdained the mindless search for gold;
She loved the woods and there took stock,
Fixed like a pine in granite rock,
By which ingrained wisdom impelled
Wilderness spirits unparalleled
Prevailing 'gainst the mickle maze
Of modern times with silent days;
Her wood-lore knowledge quickly grew
In heart an independence true;
That in her imagination,
There sparked a peregrination;
Inflamed yet some great calling;
Unknown but in a dream falling;
The wasted world all sad and lost,
No hope or prayer as the cost,
Reckoning those lakes gray or blue,
Not a flourish of life did rue…
So Ishpa Loon, which was her name,
Did with a start rise to exclaim
What she saw in the night and black,
And heard in the watery lap,
A voice mimicking a wave:
—*Ishpa, Ishpa, you must be brave.*

And Ishpa knew not what about,
Fearfully into night did shout:
—Who are you? What do you mean?
It can't be helped what can't be seen!
The wind would not answer her cries,
So Ishpa with slumberless sighs
Retreated to bed tucked in between
Her dark dream and the unforeseen...
She'd wait for light to herald day,
And by the red glow she'd steal away
To a portage in her small boat,
Cutting the engine just to float
To the shore near another lake,
And by soft foot fall she'd make
For a thicket and her canoe,
Then on the water and fair view
Of a mist shining in the sun,
She went to her nets well home-spun
Pulling for fish but there were none,
Not a bass, pike, or trout, not one;
Then setting the net as it was,
She went to the far shore because,
There was another lake she'd go,
As the wind then began to blow…
With the canoe on her shoulders,
She went along by trees and boulders,

Through the growth of an unused path,
And smelled the sweet aromatic swath,
Over a hill around a swamp,
After a mile and rugged romp
She put down the canoe where
Was a net that needed repair,
And went about to mend the net,
Then found a bay to let it set,
Where after a while with some luck
A fresh fish would redeem her pluck;
She was hungry and the tough hike –
Well she pulled, and beheld a pike!
She paddled ashore, lit a fire,
And baked her fish to her desire;
As it cooked against a flat stone,
She ate blueberries overgrown,
The rocks all so covered in blue:
Blueberries sweet her hunger true…
Her fish now done she had her fill,
Then lay down under the sun's will,
And fell asleep that afternoon,
Until called by a lonely loon,
And our breeze caressed her cheek,
Whispering, *Awake! Time to seek!*
Her eyes opened to an amber sky,
Which bade her on as 'twas time to fly…

As she paddled back to the trail,
Knowingly late to no avail,
She saw him in a birch-bark canoe,
Paddling along, but unsure who;
She had to know and went to see,
Though he seemed quite elderly…
This odd fellow lived the old way,
And she recalled what they did say,
Indeed, he was older than most,
Some believed that he was a ghost;
He hadn't appeared many a year,
Living or dead remained unclear -
Only a few knew him at all,
They said he'd come in the fall.
Ishpa had seen him at the store,
When young, at least ten years before…
He had smiled and seemed to joke,
In a cloud of tobacco smoke,
Wearing moccasins of moose leather,
Well worn and roughened from weather.
He had charisma yet pie-eyed –
A seeming purple that defied
A natural transcendence,
But in spite of independence
He was extraordinary,
If wondrous and a bit wary –

So in last light a gloaming glow,
On yet water's glimmering flow,
Ishpa drew up to say, *Hello,*
And with a wave he said, *Hello,*
She said, *I don't know you at all,*
Though I remember when but small;
I think you are a relative,
So I was told — where do you live?
—Yes, Ishpa, I remember well,
And I will tell you where I dwell.
For many moons this is my home;
He raised his arm, *And there I roam…*
Ishpa said, *You know my name;*
There's no accident that I came;
Just now I awoke from a dream,
A voice in the wind made it seem
It wanted me to seek you out,
But I don't know what it's about.
Yet here we are this summer season,
Though no idea what is the reason…
—Well, Ishpa, you are bold, I see;
A bit like me who loves being free.
There's more to this — I know the call,
The voice you heard makes many fall,
But I entrust: do not worry,
The sun has set: you should hurry.

—I'll go, but not before I know
Who you are and where you go.
—I'll camp here but be gone by morn'
I am what I am, don't be forlorn;
I've come far to collect an herb,
A holy need as aches perturb;
As nature can find a cure,
As its medicine is pure;
I don't know social benefit,
In my way the sacred must sit,
But visit if you must know more,
Aurora Lake on the far shore:
By water to the north north-west,
Thirteen days canoe I can attest.
Again a loon began to sing,
And they listened to its echoing.
—I am Makwa: heed the wild,
Take care, Ishpa, my dear child.
Then he paddled slowly away;
Ishpa sat with nothing to say;
There were thoughts heavy on her mind,
That old spirit seemed wise and kind,
Yet he lived in the bush alone –
A mystery – and now he'd gone.
She had a plan, but to bring
Some resolve was the thing.

But as destiny came to pass,
Someone spied in a looking-glass.

*

Now we leave the land of the loon,
To centers south where opportune
People live a chemical rush,
All in all a financial crush
Of material things high lifestyle,
Though we admire technical guile,
Nature effecting fabulous fate,
The universe will resonate,
A freedom in ways too profuse,
When many suffer its abuse;
Mother Nature has a golden rule:
She is a bitch who will be cruel.
Try as we might to appease gain,
Unresolved in consummate pain,
With her in mind we have ideals,
But to know that nature reveals
Healing ways all in good time,
Dark passages ever sublime…
The tragedy being no way out,

Tired, bitter we sometimes shout.
One summer day the city steamed,
The youthful crowd was tense it seemed,
There was protest a rant and rave,
Including a girl very brave,
Yelling unholy conviction,
At the G-20 malediction,
–Humans, said Mother Earth
Are innocent at birth.
So she observed from our space,
Though unevolved as a race.
Then a bad boy named John Stone,
Fire-bombed a police car unknown…
The police then arrested Sal,
The girl who was his ex-gal;
So now framed she had to pay bail,
No matter what to no avail.
All deaf ears to this mad red-head,
Though at least was released instead.
But they queried what she knew,
About the fire bomb, in fact two…
Sal now reckoned how to save face,
Thinking about it at her place;
I must get lost 'cause my life stinks,
Go north and lie low like a lynx;
Spend time on the lake with Ishpa.

—Ishpa, Ishpa, it's been such a
Long time these many years, old friend,
Let's stop time or at least pretend…
At dawn she opened the car door
Then drove away smoking to soar…
This was her requisite relief,
A diamond-rough-steal-away thief…
She flew along in celestial grace,
As we followed from intrepid space.
She didn't know that that day's news
Had sided with her boyfriend's views:
That he himself was paramount,
But innocent by his account –
Whereby they issued a warrant
Impugning Sal as abhorrent,
Who tripped now to the Grateful Dead,
Blind to trouble what lay ahead –
Down the highway free at last,
Pondered yet her wayward past:
Psychedelics had sapped
A stolen youth, drugged and trapped,
Though Sal was sunny and splendid;
Her parents died and love upended,
When their sled through the ice crashed,
And Sal orphaned – memories stashed.
Ishpa and Sal that final embrace,

The day when Sal departed their place,
Away in consequence of child laws
Commensurate to destiny's draws…
But now twenty and at the age
Realized she must turn a page –
Her life had been irrelevant,
A bit of a white elephant,
She'd been fired from a senseless job,
Landing in the unemployment mob,
Now euphoria overturned this,
As she dauntless followed her bliss:
Away from a crazed urban horde,
Healing herself so long ignored.
Now, Mother Earth plied her charm,
For those she ventured to disarm.
Sal, under her spell had to stop,
As we set in motion five o'clock;
A time to eat soup and salad,
When Sal heard him sing a ballad –
A lone hiker sat by the road
Who seemed tragic and not a toad;
Sal listened to his solemn song,
Wondering whether to take him along,
When spinning in her trance
This fellow took his chance:
–Excuse me, if I'm not too bold,

I've been waiting a half-day old,
I don't know if you're heading north,
If so, please, let me come forth.
Sal looked him up and down,
Odd, she thought with a frown,
What was he saying?
He should be playing.
—Were you not just there on that log?
—Indeed, I'm a hobo named Bob.
—A hobo, eh? So what do you do?
And where do you go? Can I trust you?
—I'm going to northern lakes supreme,
To change my life and live a dream,
I once worked the land,
Then joined a rock band,
Quit my old home,
Wrote the odd poem,
Because the wind rustled the leaves,
And ripples danced in grassy weaves;
A voice then whispered in my ear,
Yet strangely my mind did hear —
It said love lies under the sun,
The quest has already begun.
—Bob, I don't know, you're too witty,
And I'm not so sweet to have pity.
—Miss, I must confess you have grace,

But to solicit is not my place;
I beg of you, don't misunderstand,
I am true and a man of the land!
—Okay Bob, the good-natured sort,
Don't mind my defensive retort,
It feels as if some unseen guide,
Is taking us on a rum ride;
Help with gas, no dilly dally,
And by the way, the name's Sally.
Bob and Sal went their wayward way,
To Precambria, where the lake lay;
Bob spoke of life in the bush
Among the tall pines so lush –
Beaver, bear, crazy loon and moose,
White-throated sparrow, Canada goose…
Sal told him one must live with grit,
Like a misanthropic hermit;
—It's not easy when life is rough;
I know the wilderness is tough.
—Sal, don't worry, I will thrive,
As a woodsman-hunter, survive.
—Bob, you're on some quixotic trip,
If you want my advice: get a grip
On reality, stop seeking the sky;
It ain't fresh blueberry pie.
I think you should stick to singing

Something will come a-blinging.
He sang: *This girl named Sally,*
Ain't from the valley,
No mountain girl too,
Though her eyes be blue,
She's a city girl, sure,
Thinks she's tough, but demure!
—Save it Bob, I've had enough.
—Okay Sal, no need to rebuff,
I can be a bit of a tool,
But not to displease, nor a fool…
—Bob, I know just the place for you,
Near native lands north of the Sault,
I grew up there, though not to boast,
Believe me, it's a wilderness post.
They finally arrived and did park,
And found a boat just before dark.
Mother Earth smiled at that day's end,
Knowing well what was to portend.

❋

Sal went to find Ishpa at her place,
Bob remained amazed at the space:

Before him lay the land he dreamed,
Vast, awesome – how small he seemed,
He watched the sun set in the west,
A vermilion orb, he did attest:
–So sun, where's the love of my life?
Then loons cut the air like a knife,
Calling deep in his soul so strange,
Like laughing-crying an interchange,
From his heart ringing to his head,
A conundrum that seemed to wed
The lake's melodious prattle,
As dark purged the sun in battle –
A tremulous evening world,
Its ceremony unfurled.
Now sweet Ishpa and Sal embraced,
Surprise and joy in their heart's raced,
With glee in their eyes, a wonder,
Friendship remembered from asunder,
In years slipped from pubescent thought,
Now commended to each well wrought
Of womanhood, their manner and grace
Shone brilliantly in each other's face…
–Ishpa, said Sal, *My life's insane,*
I had a boyfriend who was a pain,
Then something induced a percipience,
Never known in my experience;

It seems I came here no matter what,
In spite of life becoming a rut.
I finished drama school, you know,
And worked in a small stage show,
Though promising folded before long,
Then became a waitress, which was wrong,
Something was calling in my head,
To come here seeming to be led.
—*Sal,* said Ishpa, *It happened to me,*
It's no accident that you flee,
Sometimes to follow intuition,
Is like a superstition,
Otherwise life just passes by,
Dark is earth and blue is the sky.
—*Ishpa! There is this fellow,*
He's actually quite mellow,
And built like a rock;
He's down at the dock;
He's like some wilderness swain;
What follows I can explain…
I found him way back on the road,
Looking for Mother Earth's abode,
He came from a farm,
And means no harm…
Ishpa and Sal walked to the lake,
To find Bob reclined yet awake.

He turned to look with brown eyes,
Smiling with the purple skies…
That moment a silent suspense,
Pervaded thus as no pretense,
So that their hearts had spoken –
Their stars a conjunct token,
A symmetry leading to chance,
Carrying out our divine dance…
Bob, said Ishpa, *How do you do?*
Ishpa, said Bob, *Glad to meet you.*
Just now I've heard a sacred thing;
All makes sense when the loons sing.
It seems that due to good luck,
Being here paradise just struck!
Pinch me please because I've been tricked,
Or failing that I ought to be kicked…
They all laughed in good cheer,
And felt nothing to fear;
Blessed by our intervention,
Unknown to their attention;
And henceforth our remission
Was spared getting permission;
Auguring a true kinship,
On our preeminent trip.

Two

Blue on blue of water's wave,
Lapping a delirious dream –
Aphrodite's aural nave,
Resonating her tantric theme…
Resolved to open the vault
Inducted to the hot sun,
That by virtuous default,
Wisdom threads a goddess spun –
Many faces line a gallery,
Stripped of impermanence,
A fantastic menagerie,
All attuned in ordinance…
        Enraptured to a siren,
        All nature is forgiven.

*

Early July twenty-nine,
Was cloudy with no sunshine –
Ishpa in the kitchen about,
Bob into maps quite devout,

Sal to the water a fresh swim,
All intendant to some great whim,
Bob said, *How can we be so sure?*
And Ishpa: *With no one to confer,*
I know we cannot ask,
No one must know our task,
We must disappear like a ghost,
For Makwa to comply as host,
He hinted there was much to tell,
Of medicine ways and its spell…
—But Ishpa, where is this old man?
His directions aren't worth a damn,
Aurora Lake does not exist,
So it appears foolish to persist.
—I know you might suppose this strange,
But he has cause and knows this range.
Then Sal strides in soaking wet,
—We could just as well trek Tibet!
This escapade of the unknown,
Has to be what's clearly shown
An elusive destination,
Spontaneous migration.
—But, said Ishpa, *This search is my fate,*
I'll find him if you can't relate.
—Of course, said Bob, *I'm curious,*
How else if not spurious?

Makwa's a shaman in the shield,
Like a magnet I can't but yield.
—Okay, said Sal, *Make it happen,*
Time runs on, no time for nappin'.
Now they prepared to travel –
A mystery to unravel…
A reality to heed,
Meticulously agreed
That the wild was a lonely song,
A warning easily gone wrong.
A very long time away,
Supplies needed without delay:
Extra paddles, two twenty-twos,
Tents, traps, sundry things, two canoes,
A shot gun with shot and slugs,
Tarps and nets and plastic jugs,
Utensils, axes, tump-straps, saws,
In relief of wilderness laws,
That rule with more woe than weal,
So foods like flour and meal,
And dried vegetables and beans,
Spices, sugar, salt, the means
To live in the bush a long time,
Therefore, seeds, nets, glass and lime,
A little caste stove bake oven,
All tantamount to a coven,

Of healing power to comport
Saving grace rather than abort
Intent into despair to be sure
One's troubles cannot endure.
They each kept a tin pannikin,
As well packed a wannagan.
Then came a thunderstorm
And big rain true to form.
After which were ready to leave,
Inclement weather did reprieve,
Then were given a send-off
The native folk caps did doff,
And wave in the cool north wind,
From our space couldn't rescind.

✿

They pointed west stroke upon stroke,
Now so laden they went for broke;
Three in one canoe, the second in tow,
A little awkward and a bit slow,
But they were free at last,
Having escaped the past,
From lives that had been abused,

As if each time-bomb defused
Now an all new existence,
By intrepid persistence,
Led them on to a wayward call
Far from the economy mall:
Down rivers and many a lake,
Never far from Ishpa's namesake
The ubiquitous loon nearby
That odd singular plaintive cry.
Days to weeks from sun to rain,
Summer to fall with no refrain,
The birds flew with autumn passage,
And the loons sang a sad adage...
So they listened by the warm fire,
Throwing shadows even higher
As Bobby stoked a pinewood flame,
Crackling heat cold winds untame,
Feeling frustration and no hope –
Futile like lost lifeline rope.
They'd no choice but to make a home,
Or give up and no longer roam,
The cold wind forewarned to prepare,
As winter beckoned to do or dare.
Wind and water now slip fated,
As the fire illuminated
Determined faces untold fears,

Realizing they may stay for years,
As we reckoned it would lead to this,
As they doggedly followed their bliss,
Feeling our vision from smoke and spark,
Ascending skyward like a lark.
So they decided to stay,
Ishpa saying, *We can't delay,*
We'll build a cabin for old Jack Frost,
Or succumb at a frightful cost.
On the morrow they'd find a place,
In the wild without a trace,
And hunt in this adventure,
Beyond their mad indenture,
To find Makwa they did entreat,
That never was a word defeat.
They knew Makwas territory,
Which inspired a love story:
It so happened those past three weeks,
Bobby and Ishpa exchanged peeks –
Love like water finds what it seeks,
Filling cracks and blind to critiques;
No matter what cast from above,
We can never predict true love;
In their stars was a special blend –
A composite love without end;
On that night Sal took the cue,

Fibbing that her period was due...
Our smitten sat near each other,
Trying to say I'll be your lover,
Yet fearful of taking the plunge,
As to render an awkward lunge,
In that the penultimate sport,
A misapprehension in report,
Vied a reluctance to impose,
The nectar scent and thorny rose…
Such that they seemed convulsive,
As their hearts became impulsive,
And could no more suppress desire,
Having stirred a mighty fire…
They sipped herbal Labrador tea,
The cure for their choked repartee;
Ishpa finally laughed,
Bobby just sitting daft,
—Last one in is a rotten egg!
But jumping she tripped on a peg,
And lay there quietly in pain,
Bobby comforting in vain.
She seemed hurt when in a flash
She kissed him in a wild mash
And they made love – a fumbling pair,
Doubling up in the northern air,
Wherefore consummation reigning,

Until morning when Sal complaining,
Unzipped the libidinous nest,
Beseeching them to now attest
Her helpless situation,
And remedy privation.

*

The Loons, so-called, now for fun,
Knew not they were on the run,
By an investigative plea
Spear-headed by agent Orley,
Who had an axe to grind
With a bush-whackers mind.
The Loons thought they found a lake,
Thinking it the proverbial cake,
So they went along a rough track,
Then Bob went back for the last pack;
Standing on shore he saw the plane
Land up-wind on its water lane,
To then motor where Bob stood.
Out came a pilot wearing a hood,
He asked gruffly for Sal McCoy,
Flicked his badge which did annoy

Bobby, who had nothing to say,
Taken aback that fateful day…
—I want to see who you're with,
She left with a guy woodsy as pith,
And a native girl Ishpatina,
Whom I gather's no ballerina.
Showing his gun he motioned ahead,
Urging Bobby, who full of dread
Hatched a plan, so began to talk:
—You know, officer, not to balk,
But you'd do with some courtesy,
Or else one reacts purposely…
He feigned to stumble and picked a rock,
And in a flash gave Orley a knock.
The agent down, Bob with all speed
Alarmed his friends with little heed;
Away they went from this bad turn,
Being forced now to slash and burn
Their very strange innocent trip
Fixed fickle fate and did a flip –
For a while keeping to the trees,
Lighting no fire, though they did freeze,
And when they awoke more early,
Or to keep on at dusk unclearly –
Paramount they'd not be seen,
Undercover of sylvan green;

Carried on in a silent dream,
Where one lake there led a stream,
That finally found their spot,
Paradise more home than not:
The cold water teemed with fish,
And flora and fauna every wish –
The mysterious Aurora Trout,
Wallowed in pools all about –
Reds, purples, orange, shiver,
Flashing red-gold darting to quiver...
They chose level ground out of the wind,
And assembled what they could find
To build a cabin of pine trunks,
And chinked with mud-lime chunks;
The roof made from split cedar rails,
Shakes and birch-bark with little nails,
Bob made a pine floor, smooth it was cut,
Even a thick door sealed tight when shut.
Sal and Ishpa gazed at Bob's class,
Packed in the woodstove panes of glass,
To make a window on each side,
Airtight with cedar wood-slat guide…
These hardy travelers from afar,
Between them did adversity bar,
While Ishpa tended nets and traps,
Cured pelts, smoked fish, food under wraps.

From fall to winter the water froze,
All about work the life they chose.
One day snaring rabbits, they found
A cave with a bear underground:
They took its life to save their own,
Because its uses were well known –
A fur blanket and oil for a lantern,
And the meat followed the pattern
Thus to use nature was their choice,
Paying all heed to Mother Nature's voice.
So winter passed, Ishpa with child,
Snug they were with firewood piled,
And wondered if Makwa lived nearby,
As this country did not belie,
The way the wind swirled,
Or how the clouds twirled,
Yet they could not find their mentor,
Resigned to winters bad temper…
In spite of being so happy together,
They survived the inclement weather.

❋

Yet one April morning's thaw,

35 ～

Starvation seemed nature's law,
When food supplies did not abound,
The ice unstable and unsound,
And the land's impassable bush,
Because the snow had turned to slush...
The Loons rationed what food they had,
For weeks it was so very bad,
Outside the windows water would drip,
Seeming to end their quixotic trip,
When it dawned they were going to die,
That morning Ishpa did espy
In a blanket of snow a footprint,
And followed along taking the hint
That something amazing, so droll,
Led over a distant knoll -
Now the Loons were in a kind of shock,
As they climbed up on this big rock,
Where the prints vanished, just ended,
Like a ghost with them befriended.
But in the crystal sun below,
They beheld three moose all aglow.
Bobby then shot the bull down,
His true aim had struck its crown.
The other moose did disappear,
When they whooped up a blessed cheer –
Thanks to their four-legged brother,

Who gave life for the Great Mother…
Later, having eaten a meal,
They wondered what was so surreal:
—Those footprints in the snow weren't ours!
That mystery just ate the hours…
—It must've been something alien,
Said Sal, *Or unknown mammalian,*
No matter we must be grateful,
No matter how strange or fateful.
So when the ice melted that spring,
They set out and went exploring;
Having searched a circumference,
Ten miles deep in reference
To view a distant high hill,
They climbed with sure-footed will,
To gaze from the rocky summit
A world that seemed to plummet;
Their eyes casting a silent pitch,
Desolate, but about to switch
That invisible we fly
By our skimming by,
In a sudden draft to sniff
A most miraculous whiff -
The aroma of smoke,
Inhaled like a toke…
They scampered down that rugged side,

Wildly stirred and watery-eyed,
To a lake where stood an old log house,
And emerged a man they did arouse;
Indeed, 'twas Makwa looking about,
Eyeing the Loons hearing them shout…
He smiled seeing Ishpa and her friends,
Now quiet to make amends,
As if imposing by denial,
'Til Makwa remarked on their guile,
—Ishpa Loon, welcome,
And friends, to my home.
Ishpa introduced Bob and Sal,
Who felt strange, supernatural;
They wondered about his age,
How he appeared like a sage.
Makwa amused with their adulation,
Remained calm with his admiration.
—One day my story you shall hear;
But for the moment let us cheer.
I commend what you have achieved,
Though these portents have been conceived,
In spirit by way of the wind,
Travelling lands no one can find,
You see, this sanctuary,
Is extraordinary,
That to the world is errant,

Because of something aberrant.
And with his hand he swept the sky,
And that moment I appeared on high...
–*But now,* he said, *Let's have some tea;*
And I'll hear your tale, patiently.
Makwa beckoned in a way brisk,
As to keep from them our disc,
His eye turned away in a blink,
Incommensurate with our link.

*

In his cabin one lived the past,
As if time was newly recast:
Items were exquisitely made,
Considered relics, lore waylaid:
Objects therein showed skills long out-fazed,
As if time was mnemonically razed:
Bark cups, traps, a quiver, bow and arrow,
Pelts on a toboggan long and narrow -
Also some ancient artifacts:
Obsidian points, adzes, stone axe,
All things served to interpolate
A netherworld-like magic state –

A rite-de-passage metaphor
That modern life can't underscore.
They sipped their tea and told their tale -
Makwa, his ear tuned to the grail,
Of our imposed orchestration,
Outstanding manifestation;
Fain to reveal what he did feel,
Knowing truth an Achilles' heel…
The Loons told of the moccasin mark,
That constrained him not to embark,
Pleading ignorance then relent,
Considering their time well spent:
—I know not the need for a sign
As to the goodness of the wine,
But in your experience
Beware a prurience —
Mother Nature has her way with things,
What, I cannot say, but ripple rings.
Perplexed, the Loons thought he knew,
Yet Makwa seemed stuck as in glue.
Yet impressed by his erudition,
Notably his good condition:
They guessed eighty – perhaps too much…
Anon, spring and summer passed as such,
A time so blessedly lived in mirth,
At which, full term, Ishpa gave birth

To a fine boy who long forsworn,
As Felix, for her twin stillborn.
Ishpa and child well – they all sighed,
And wind in the trees now complied.
Mak made a tekanagan papoose,
Saying, *Moss diapers shouldn't be loose!*
Now autumn in their domicile,
Their existence did reconcile
With a hardy predilection,
To an instinctive perfection
Through Makwa's wilderness life,
That helped to lessen patent strife.
They dried raspberries, dogberries, blue,
Starflowers, wild rice, muckeegoba too;
Bob made his first birchbark canoe,
Though without Makwa hadn't a clue.
Alas, we nurtured our wild brood,
Likened to nature's holy rood.

Three

In the wild we draw out the loon –
We are their guardian sphere,
Conducting symphonies to the moon,
Be as it may without a peer…
Ponder the haunting dissonance,
Across water and rocky shores,
Subliminal in innocence,
The call of miraculous mores:
Subsumed in our vernacular,
Echoing sad human folly –
Intonations spectacular,
To decry its viral volley.
       Survival we offer,
       By the love we proffer.

✳

The harvest moon on the morrow,
A north wind numbing like sorrow,
But for the warm fire that night,
Urged Makwa to purge his plight:

Something till now suppressed –
Strange spirits dispossessed,
Like a rustle in the trees,
Or shrieking gull on the breeze.
The Loons looked on as the fire danced,
Into purplish eyes when Ishpa chanced
A query about those prints in the snow,
To untie his tongue so his tale did flow:
—You wonder right that I know of her,
Only to attest the Great Mother,
In that she is wise but fickle,
Like a child but agèd mickle.
So what I'm about to explain,
You must not think I'm insane.
Turning to each, then to him,
The Loons twisted on a limb –
The revelation bid wonder,
Intelligence did plunder,
Compounded by his old age,
One hundred-thirty, a mage
Inclined to antiquity,
With incredulity:
—Of my birth on this lake in this wood,
Is a history that I made good:
Ishpa, we met a year ago,
In fact, before you did know

I was led by spirits strong,
Not knowing if right or wrong;
The signs had then become chronic,
When the loons became symphonic;
Yet even then did I hesitate,
Not wanting to upset your fate,
For I am not what you think I am,
Which puts me in a bit of a jam -
I'm at the age to cease caring
'Bout the secret of my bearing:
Ishpa, Sal, Bob, even Felix,
Take heed of nature's tricks:
Reason is something to beware,
Because of those little tracks there,
In spite of their induction,
Yet belying its conduction…
I do not know what lies in store —
Something lethal or divine whore,
Not that she is of vile variety,
Rather super-human propriety;
Alas, she is my birth mother,
Who resides in a sphere called Zephyr —
And moves about in the wind,
Whose presence always did rescind.
Now the Loons had been well prepared,
Notwithstanding how they'd been spared:

—What, they cried, *You're her child?*
Sal then declared, *This is too wild!*
Makwa sat there with his head down,
The Loons looked on in a wry frown.
—The truth is I am half-human —
Think about my long life span…
What of these purple eyes?
Do they tell so many lies?
Had I told you this the first day,
Well, what then would you say?
I've never met her; she doesn't age;
My father told me and he was a sage.
Tebishkopeshoo was his name,
He lay with her and felt no shame;
She bore me here where they dwelt,
But left before the ice did melt,
Yet still held in great veneration,
A legend from my generation -
A myth not easy to explain,
In keeping with our sacred domain.
There's no telling what will become;
There's never been a rule of thumb.
She appeared before in silk robes,
With diamonds in her earlobes;
Apparently not religious,
Though perversely prodigious

In the sense of philosophy
As a kind of idolatry –
In herself – her dark auburn hair –
A beauty beyond compare –
I was told she appeared twenty,
A natural being with plenty
Of excellent features,
The strangest of creatures –
Telling she was synthetic,
And sexually athletic;
I don't underwrite this meaning;
I've never seen something seeming
Synthetic, in fact, I don't know the word;
One of you, perhaps, by the way has heard.

The Loons could only stare at Mak
In awe, as he looked calmly back,
As now he seemed more at ease,
Legs crossed hands on his knees:
–Now time, I think, is opportune;
She may come to spell fortune,
As tomorrow is the full moon.
At this time gather many a loon,
Before their journey down south,
And sing as though from one mouth;
And at this time I sense something fair,
Something sightless, floating on air;

Even now, she is listening,
Even here, eyes glistening;
Raven! he called into night,
—I, Makwa, your son and light,
Has all these years upheld our ways,
And will, till the skies final days;
And you, Zephyrus, invisible,
Show me what's indivisible;
Whose visage is nature's backdrop
Whether seen bottom or top;
Trees, rocks, lakes, stars, perfect cover,
An anti-gravity hover;
Turning florescent blue or pink,
To change in a chameleon blink;
Thus Raven had forsaken me so,
And Zephyr like the wind did go —
Am I not your loyal friend?
Will you now condescend?
I know she's here though can't tell,
As in dark we can't see well;
Nor how she lives in a space ship,
But she's on my radar blip;
I don't know what it does mean,
Recalled since I was a teen.
I know what I know and don't surmise,
I tell you true as the sun does rise.

Sal then gave Makwa a quick kiss,
Proceeding to say how remiss
Raven had been many a year,
Surfing the skies in Zephyr's sphere.

＊

Night wore on while they wondered,
And by the fire in silence pondered;
Felix asleep at Ishpa's feet,
Sal basked in the pinewood heat:
—Makwa, let's face it, we're a bit dazed;
Yet I believe you're not at all crazed.
This dark Raven, who's caused you stress;
How's it that she's so comfortless?
—Sal, said Ishpa, *it's time to conform;*
All what we know is that it's not the norm,
What's unnatural is still nature,
No matter how odd its stature.
—There's much that we don't know, said Bob.
As the fire hissed from a pine gob.
Makwa spoke out of his reverie,
Like smoke ascending upwardly:
—Don't pity me, I know my life;

Somewhat blessed with a sacred strife,
Passed down to me from my forbearers,
It's my honour to tend many cares.
I'm proud to work with my hands,
Though the tribe's gone to distant lands.
That was long ago, but here I stay;
What father said I feel to this day:
He said know that you have power;
Guard the earth's most precious flower;
No part of life is she unaware,
To the particles of thin air;
Not just earth, but humanity too,
Thousands of years on this ball blue.
He said I was a great conception,
Semi-synthoid with no exception —
An alien serving to leaven,
And pander a kind of heaven…
Yet, all I am is a shaman,
Cast in the wild as an orphan.
Who learned natural law,
As seamless without flaw,
What the world deems to be God,
But misunderstood if a bit odd;
Because people use it as their own,
And reap whatever they have sown,
Like mythology that won't die,

As a collective dream on high;
Like the morning sun alighting the pines,
What reason radiates the heart outshines
The humdrum of life's incipience,
Transcending our best percipience…
Raven named me Little Bear,
Then disappeared into thin air;
And if you find this hard to take,
Imagine solitude on this lake,
Excuse me for living these dreams,
All is not what it sometimes seems.
I was told there's a synthetic man
Who is some kind of chieftain,
Who was called Crow,
As far as I know;
And lives near the Dog Star,
Where they came from afar…
Their forbearers were like human,
And went extinct of some condition,
That made their entire race sterile,
Leaving the Synthoids to their peril…
They are neo-aboriginal,
Pseudo-native subliminal,
Living many a millennial
Age seemingly perennial,
Super-impressed in their exile,

Our world as an ideal domicile.
Makwa paused to poke a red ember
Under the moonlight of September.
The cool night enveloped a haze,
Soon to free them from our maze…
Bob said, *This is all too surreal,*
We need time to let it congeal,
My mind threatens disbelief,
In the wanting of relief;
So my philosophy as the theme,
Begs the milk maid dispense the cream;
As to subscribe to the above,
Her hermetic exotic love…
—Bob, let's infer her virility,
Inspires love-defying futility,
In that her omnipotence,
Decries some incompetence…
My father said, tempted of vice,
Once converted, she was the spice,
But nonetheless careful and wary,
Disdaining earth because it's scary.
—Makwa, said Sal, *Can she be true?*
The more I know the more I rue!
Can one who so exploits life
Be great, yet so terrible wife?
It seems to me that we are doomed

If Mother Nature keeps us marooned,
Needless to say, I would do more,
At least show herself at our door.
Makwa said, *I think she would concur:*
But our being not so great is not sure;
To forsake love begs not pity,
Strife is our nitty gritty.
Sal replied, *Such is humanity,*
Better than prey on our vanity.
Bob said, *She's had us much beguiled;*
For all we know she's been defiled.
–Perhaps, said Sal, *Misogyny,*
Primitive man, sick progeny...
–Raven, said Bob, *Gives us hope,*
At least yet to interlope,
We should be more than grateful,
Rather than incline as hateful.
–Yes, said Ishpa, *She's not a harlot,*
More the quintessential starlet;
We can't disrespect what we don't know,
Mak just said: one reaps what they sow,
Patience rules virtue, not ignorance,
So let privilege take a chance:
And not question what's wrong or right,
We must be cautious with insight;
One thing's certain, she's ingenuous,

And whatever fortune, be it tenuous,
This Sisyphean thing — this wingless bird,
Has in Raven a power unheard;
We see but an airbrushed picture,
And fear works a porno-scripture;
It is the way that forces collide,
So we are chosen to climb the divide
Of that netherworld mountain peak,
From which the sky sits at our feet,
To look at earth under the sun,
And see many a shadow spun,
Feeling in our mantle every part,
How I shudder to feel her heart.

Four

Of earth we're the sphere of heaven,
Peerless in view of all that see,
Or to hear our music leaven
Ripples of human symmetry…
The mystery of this pannakin,
A fountain of youth will suffice,
Ever-living that mannequin –
Mother of God phœnix of vice…
Clung to being on blue ball earth,
Ancient myth embodied, approved,
Her reason in a hybrid birth,
A reality ever-removed...
Like Isis all else belies
The truth behind purple eyes.

*

The next evening, the moon full,
The Loons anxious, felt its pull,
Sitting, staring, onto the lake,
Distant, letting their supper bake:

Fresh trout with herbs and starflowers.
Makwa too, was silent for hours,
Then eating in the crystalline cool,
A distant loon trilled to mock a fool,
Its echo crying in their hearts
Across the evening sky that starts
The purple curtain to the world
Now descended as stars unfurled -
Smokey air and a lone wolf bark
Made havoc from the fire's spark,
Piqued a tension now wound
Portending something bound
To happen as they sat impressed,
Bearing down on them a light no less –
Hearts tremulous in thumping chest
Pre-empting fate's prophetic quest:
Searing deep a postulation
Of an unknown adulation,
Became as one the loon vocals,
Emitting from opened portals,
Of past and present harmonics,
All rushing like narcotics,
They trilled in cacophony.
Sal now stood verily to see
Over the horizon the light
A blue florescence in the night

Taken like a neon-libation,
Tears fell in their sublimation,
Bob and Ishpa froze in shock,
Makwa stood as passive as rock.
'Twas I, Zephyrus, on my own,
If a little gloried renown,
Making slow advance,
Dazzling to entrance
The loons to a pitched elation,
As a synchronized ovation,
Benumbed in miraculous mirth,
A revolution in birth…
Then darkness like a spent flash,
All now quiet but for a splash
Like something in the lake swimming,
When out stepped a naked girl grinning,
Dripping wet without any shame –
Childish, as if playing some game,
But her audience sat prone, supine,
And seeing their fear, she said, *I am benign…*
I know my intrusion
Begets confusion
About this haven;
Just call me Raven.
So they beheld her sacredness
Gaping at blatant nakedness.

—You know, she said, *I'm a moth to a light,*
Notwithstanding how it beholds my plight:
Let me with the truth regress,
With no attempt to impress,
That from the dawn of history,
My renown came clandestinely;
The object of many an idol,
Not to effect any such tidal
Infamy — but now I'm free…
Liberated, as can be —
Please bear with my obloquy,
And you may begin to see.
Don't mind the paucity of attire,
Nature is heedless to require;
I have a particular karma —
My metaphorical dharma
Plummets the Abyssinian abyss…
Then straight away gave Makwa a kiss.
The Loons dumbstruck could barely conceive
What their eyes seemed to all but deceive;
Makwa seemed crushed by this foray,
And got down on his knees to pray.
—Up Makwa, she bid, *My ablution*
Proffers only absolution
To expiate my lost bond to you,
I ask your pardon as I'm true —

If you could know my objective,
You'd understand my perspective;
It's a fulsome tale that can wait,
Until after we acclimate -
The sufferance that does ferment,
Once imbibed suffuses lament:
Down through the ages to this day,
Evil forces retain their sway,
It is they who cause all the funk —
In love and kindness they debunk,
And assuredly throw stones
At utopia which postpones,
Our universal resonance,
Because of moral ignorance:
So they stumble along
In an unholy throng,
That darkness bespeaks the adage:
Under the sun is most savage.
We must be open, circumspect —
Dishonesty, we must reject;
My wisdom is a conjecture,
Though last and least to lecture.

Becoming quiet she looked around;
Her glances did all the more confound,
Insomuch no one ventured to speak,
As Raven made them feel quite meek;

A lingering shock still repressed,
To which Raven now processed,
'Til Sal's spurious sense restored
Equilibrium from being floored
Who being so sillily simple
Erupted like a bad pimple:
—I don't mind that you don't wear clothes,
I just wonder what you propose;
What on earth are we supposed to feel?
You're amazing, but what's the deal?
Raven then replied, Sal, let us thrive
By the medicinal cure of your jive;
Between you all there's synergy,
Yes, like a clairvoyant clergy,
But not a religion to spin
Harkened belief thinking to win,
When all is sick by blood-letting
Invoking God in fervid fretting,
Seemingly immortal ever;
When in fact not at all clever;
You see thus how people smitten,
Must abide by what's been written;
Yet again, the disparate poor
Suffer under an icon or Moor.
So I'll tell to your heart's delight;
But first, Zephyrus, in the night

Waits to meet you out in the dark –
Come Zephyr! Show yourself and park…
I, of course, flashed florescent blue,
Then suddenly vanished from view,
Appearing then to emanate,
As a true miraculous mate,
Showing off under the moon's shaft,
The most intrepid spheroid craft,
If I don't say so to myself,
Penning my penultimate pelf…
Bobby Sparrow exclaimed: *Gravity*
Seems not to sink the cavity!
A most terrific twilight
That was ever brought on by night…
–Bobby, said Raven, *He is that diverse,*
And yours throughout the universe,
Any galaxy, star system, perforce,
With one condition, ignorance divorce –
You must be visionary,
Not a mad missionary;
We use electromagnetic propulsion
Generating a kind of emulsion –
Artificial gravity is the way,
The difference between night from day,
Comparing natural gravity and ours,
Which out-of-phase harnesses powers,

Amplifying the fourth dimension,
Where surfing space in suspension,
Or floating on air will persist
A new paradigm with a twist,
In that the leap is gigantic,
Like a man to jump the Atlantic
Instantly, so your behavior
Must be cool like a savior —
Well, nonetheless, that's how it goes,
By separating neutrinos,
Where a fissure of which could bust
Like an egg and crack the Earth's crust.
Feel Zephyr's hull, it will dispel
Skeptical notions and repel
Your touch, though nothing can be seen
Because beneath his skin a screen
Mimics transparency as real
And in such a way will conceal
Around, below, above, a mirage
A simulated camouflage;
You see, we're unseeable,
Which we find agreeable.
Bob then asked, *What is your fuel?*
—Our main factor, a dense jewel
Fires a reactor which the intent
Converts this heavy element

Into such a powerful force,
It's a renewable resource
Emitting no radiation –
The supreme creation…
Around Zephyr's perimeter,
We control the inhibitor,
And with a pulse are propelled
Through any slipstream impelled
In the fissure of warped motion –
Speed, a superfluous notion –
Travelling space not all that distant,
When it curves back in an instant,
So we hitch a ride
To the other side…
This way we hop as a ship must tack
Off to Xaras, our home, there and back
Where lives the last man, Crow,
Who came here once but did forego…

*

I, Zephyrus, invisible.
Remain the indivisible,
Now shone a soft, comfortable light,

Whose radiance lit up the night,
Leading to my hatch,
As to strike a match –
So Raven came in well composed
Though the Loons were little disposed
To enter my numinous void,
Looking and feeling paranoid…
But once in, sealed shut, I lifted
Over the lake and slowly drifted
Over Precambria
Sounding an aria –
The music of Orpheus' lyre
Resurrected from love's pyre,
Serenading what they saw
Through my virtual maw,
More like our surrounding monitor
Like windows the sum compositor
Of technology long ago forged,
Before we were from Xaras disgorged,
To wander across the sea of space,
Until we found this beautiful place,
Home for one of the last of our race,
The others gone without a trace…
But now let us look inside
Where Raven does reside:
Smooth rocks, flowers, and a spring,

An eddy pool – a wondrous thing:
For my system's hydrology,
In parallel cosmology
Metaphorically unique,
Defies any camp critique.
Here we have ancient curios
From long gone scenarios:
Many a rare manuscript,
Compelled by those to encrypt;
Sundry mementos,
In time to disclose,
An antiquitous fixture,
Like the odd movie picture,
When Raven befriended as Isis
Cleopatra at an early crisis,
Bereft in a sea of sand,
Before Caesar came to land;
And so she mentored Cleopatra –
She was keen on the Kama Sutra –
Besides this stuff from the ages,
Work given us by the mages:
Poems and paintings some unsung,
Scattered about all unhung;
Ancient jewelry anthropocentric,
A classic trove of style eccentric –
Diamonds, sapphires, rubies and gold,

Treasures given from suitors of old;
Then her cozy cushioned marble bed,
Covers with fleece pillows for her head,
Toilet and wardrobe all so crafted,
And a kitchen long since drafted.
My windows surround the interior
Showing earth descend to the exterior;
The sun flared above the horizon,
A bright orange magenta upon
The margin of the twilit planet,
As we watched her intent gaze set
Beyond the sun illuminated,
Eyes, happy-sad accentuated
An emanation so striking,
A strange surreal liking
That her paranormal duty
Must conform to such beauty:
Lithe, supple, and so exquisite,
Her pearl-drop bottom requisite
To delicacy in all her parts:
Arms, fingers, legs, stymied the arts
To depict her physiology,
Engendering mythology –
Her maker out-performed nature –
Appearing thus in stature,
A creature so rare,

That brought on despair
At her pale opalescent skin,
Forswearing original sin…
Her languid motion bound one check
Her dark raven locks down her neck…
Further still, no blemish, or body hair,
Attended ruby nipples firm, and fair,
Her breasts, though small,
Did all enthrall…
Her electric aura would stun,
As one blinded by the sun –
Soulful amethyst eyes
Caused many a demise…
Her nose, chin and brow, sage, but soft,
Wine-red lips that held one aloft –
And down to the nether power,
Her chalice and tender flower
Budding pubescent pink –
Her deep genetic link,
Engendered for age-long life,
For good or ill a patent strife,
Her ubiquitous means to entrance,
But now dressed to make an advance…
In faded jeans and a t-shirt,
She turned with a look almost pert,
If all could see her endearing face,

Eye to eye, forever not a trace
Of malcontent be found on earth,
Such was this being of utter worth,
Though envy's sting,
From ripples ring…
—So here we are in my abode;
A bit simple not to out-mode
Post-modern style, I must confess,
I'm reclusive like an abbess —
My bondage all my history,
Perusing doors — no exit free;
Beauty can be such a terrible curse,
This face equated with a cherry purse —
A flower blooming that will not die,
Like nature's most delicious pie;
No matter that my illusions
Are interminable delusions
That my well-earned humanity,
Waxed from alien vanity
Innocently intertwined
Immortally inclined;
Sometimes with drastic consequence,
Adding ill fame to my offense —
For in retrospect I'm a girl,
Having found the penitent pearl
Of wisdom as an over-sexed deity,

Embodying spontaneity…
I could not stay in places long,
For fear of the ignoble throng —
I had been in Numidia
And changed my name to Lydia,
Then for a good while in Corinth
Plying the sensual labyrinth
Where all the world came for love —
The temple's goddess above
The very fame of ultimate lust,
That I found the consummate bust…
Then became an ascetic,
As a holy hermetic
Of a woman's order in northern Greece,
Where the bereft and abused found peace…
But one day a man spoke named Paul,
As all were gathered in the hall,
About the Word of God — a King,
Who offered an Engagement Ring
To a woman as his equal,
Admitted in fact a sequel,
From whom Yeshua the Essene,
Had been married to the Magdalene,
Queen Miriam of the Nazarene,
When that schism did intervene —
Her marriage all in disharmony —

She'd have none of Paul's apostasy

That she left Yeshu forthwith,

Forsaking him to his myth,

And exiled herself to France,

Deprived of her true romance,

Yet their dynastic creed,

Once vouchsafed to breed…

And so given the chance,

I spurned my damnéd dance,

Having transcended Aphrodite

Into something less flighty,

Yet the delicious cherry,

Was no longer that very

Promiscuous holy bitch,

But rather a sweet pious witch,

Empowered in the King out there,

He chose me with purposed prayer;

I know the whole story,

Subsumed in his glory;

Paul married us the next day,

An antidote to decay…

Raven then asked their pardon

And prepared tea from her garden,

Then picked up Felix on the bed,

Held to her chest before she said,

Little one, my descendant child,

What a life you'll lead in the wild.
Sal said, *This is inscrutable,*
Rather more incomputable!
Raven said, *Some called me slut,*
But I loved all life incorrupt;
Fate's a rhinoceros,
The point: preposterous.
With that Sal slipped into the pool,
And sputtered, *I've learned the rule:*
Never challenge the Great Mother,
And for good measure her brother;
They take the proverbial cake,
And eat it up for goodness sake!
Raven then flipped a drachma,
And then looked at old Makwa –
Tears of joy running down his face;
But joy with sorrow did displace
His countenance he held so well,
As Raven thought it best to tell
Of misgivings and her presence,
Knowing love was of the essence…
–Makwa, your father told you
Before dying of that flu,
Of all things that he'd come to see,
The most auspicious being me,
With the import of this knowledge,

With your tribe forged a wedge,
When the government moved the band,
And you determined to save the land,
Amidst looming dissipation,
You held fast to your station;
Because of me you stayed behind
Honoring the legacy of our kind;
You then worked for a surveyor,
Guiding, and became purveyor
Of supplies which made me proud,
But I couldn't remove the shroud
Since my presence might cause a mire,
That I know would not expire…
And here is the crux of the tale
My husband, Yeshu, did not fail,
In that his promise of faith,
Was restored by my wedding wraith,
In the belief of a messiah,
But people had deemed him pariah,
Heeded by strict protocol
When he chose to take the fall,
Because he ordained the Gentile
Among his own rank and file,
Who rejected his resurrection
As doctrine implying his election -
This systemic persecution,

Prescribed in execution,
Then to rise from the dead,
And rule as it was read;
Alas, Yeshu, died not for sins,
In spite of how the myth begins;
In fact he was saved from death,
Simulated to a last breath
By hemlock sponged to his lips,
Purged later from these grips,
In a Dead Sea cave
Thought to be his grave;
It all happened about Qumran,
Co-opted as Jerusalem
Whose ploy had turned out for the worst,
The later church bid the dam burst,
To cut down the last girl and boy,
Condemned by those He did annoy -
They hated the desposyni,
His blood-relative progeny.
They enforced Yeshu as God,
And deemed his bloodline fraud;
Yet honest, enlightened, and true,
That two thousand years can't undo:
But the irony kills -
Rivers of bloody spills!
The tortures, burnings and horror!

In the name of a holy explorer!
The fault I too held accountable,
For the hate was insurmountable…
Humanity runs deeper than him
As Mother Nature's homonym -
Cruel are antiquitous laws,
Glacial in presient thaws.
So, Makwa, where I was needed most,
Reprove me from your lonely post.
—Great Mother, do not bereave so,
For no matter how it did go;
I had faith in natural will,
I kept this land, which I keep still.
In my heart I knew you would come,
By the command of the dictum,
My forefather, Hannioyeh, inducted,
That our line has faithfully conducted;
And Felix will one day take the torch,
No matter how hot the sun will scorch,
Or Ishpa, depending on my demise,
Or how longevity does improvise.
—Likewise, Makwa, that's why I'm here;
Almost five thousand years, I fear,
This Synthoid will not be long around,
As mortal life is something profound,
In that it will be my final passion,

My propinquity in living fashion;
As poetry is substantial,
But not overly financial,
But do not heed my inference,
Not that it makes a difference.
—Okay, said Sal, Not to be rude;
But that's one hell of a prelude!
—Sal, let me begin my story;
Not to be too oratory;
Five thousand years is a long time,
Both honey sweet and bitter lime:
Terrible lessons I did learn,
Evolved in ways my heart did burn:
In the annals of love I haunt,
Looming in the shadows gaunt,
A visage peers a bit like me,
Living with all humanity…
I mean to sow a fine suture,
And heal the sick for the future;
You see life regenerates life
Universally known as strife;
So what beckons without ado,
Chides my innocence through and through,
To the point I'm afraid for earth,
To give something of greater worth;
Since Yeshu was no antidote,

And disdained a church to promote,
The least of which becomes a pope,
As Yeshu gave personal hope —
A God within to contemplate
All heart, or else we abdicate.
This was his scrupulous concern
But few others could this discern,
Except Miriam, me, his wife,
Whose enemies hounded all our life
When they co-opted pagan fervor
For the universal preserver;
In that man emulated God,
As if their words a lightning rod —
Fundamental fools professed death,
Holding all to their fiery breath,
As in nature their duty down
To negatives with a mad frown;
Evolution will reconcile
Good and bad of the rank and file:
As victors will assume the right,
No matter how impaired their sight —
Take me, their living mannequin,
Long survived in Zephyr's pannikin,
Long sought on this terraqueous reach,
Manhandled as a juicy peach:
I observed all and heard the sounds

Of their ranting within my bounds,
So permeating like warm rain,
Seeking the answer to our pain
I classified much of nature,
Rock and plant, culture and creature;
Unknown was not one entity
Except our serenity:
And to this day, I've tried to find
The secret key that dodged my mind,
In spite of human history,
Its very truth — a mystery...
Not just why, for facts are quite real,
But nothing summates what one can feel.
In this secret assumes a God,
Though nescient with me I can laud
The idea as means to an end,
Honest belief all will defend.

※

Raven stood a moments respite,
Sipping tea to watch the twilit
Sun peep a raging scarlet,
Across the earth for our starlet -

Then to orbit in gentle rush,
The Loons peered down all a-hush,
Seeing the huge blue marble ball,
Turning round as they felt small.
Standing near the crystalline screens,
Looking at stars beyond the means
Of existence in remote space,
That blueball earth must now embrace…
—Everyone loves a shining star,
Whether close or from afar,
All the world is their very own,
No matter what or over-blown,
There is nothing I do not crave,
Love, money, or self-made slave…
Though no use for hypocrisy,
I so despise autocracy -
Nature reigns over our ascendance,
No matter what our transcendence:
Light and dark interchanged,
A lightning spark deranged
Neptune's illumination
Dooms every temptation…
Throughout time I've had great friends,
All lost to fate — all mortal ends.
From Asia to Afric,
I've lived soulful traffic,

From dearest love to gross intent,
My will to love was eminent —
A shadow-show of dire import,
So availed of such a sport;
From a harvest-hope so conjoined,
The seed of many so purloined;
They could not perceive my desire;
My hormones were a bit haywire,
Having a sumptuous instinct,
Barren of race almost extinct,
The last of us hoping to be bred,
Naïve in habit — horny in the head;
A catalyst to survival,
Virility as my idol;
Whereof true chemistry,
Understood, wasn't free,
Yet mishaps bore wisdom from folly,
Bittersweet and melancholy.
Of coitus I became jealous
Of people more zealous,
In the heart of love my vice,
So never too steep the price,
Pointing the hand of destiny,
Not realizing my infamy;
As I gathered along time's track
Unconditional love went crack —

Genetics from rock and dust,
Once arrived like a rocket thrust -
Star-kissed extraterrestrials we are,
Eyes to heaven come from afar;
A blue ball hurtling through space,
Nourished from fire all one race…
Let me indulge you in a moment -
Not meaning to generate foment,
We can recreate living beings
From mnemonic virtual screens…
From people since passed away,
Come alive as in their day —
Then earth's view now quickly vanished,
Replaced by someone looking famished
Fasting beside a clear stream;
With shining eyes a dream
In charismatic behavior
A natural born savior,
Water tumbling ad delirium,
As he rises in his imperium…
—Look, she said, *Hey Siddhartha,*
How's my wise holy llama?
Presiding in your great glory,
Come, dear, let's hear your story;
Tell my friends your wayward way.
He looks at her without delay:

–Kali, it's very good to see you.
His eyes reveal an emerald hue.
–You're not alone, he said from his side.
And introducing them fit to be tied
Sal entranced to the screen did touch,
He likewise, saying: *It's a bit much.*
–No kidding, said Sal, *Are you the Buddha?*
No, just a hermit, Siddhartha.
–But you seem alive inside the screen!
–True, as you, but Kali's world between,
Since you are flesh, yet I'm sentient,
In myself with a technical penchant
To Kali, who granted me this wish:
Bestowing my speech in good English;
You know, she once wagered a bet
I can never profess regret
That I would be the chosen one
For all time under the sun
For a dilly-dally in our tree,
Observed by a meddling monkey
Called Buddha the Enlightened,
Joking thus she made me frightened;
I did not believe what she did perpend,
Yet transformed me into legend,
But she'd remain anonymous,
With her presence synonymous

With some intrepid on-goings
As those imbedded to her loins,
Such as Yeshu the Nazerene,
My friend with the orthodox lean...
Then the monkey jumped and landed
Near Siddhartha, who demanded
His companion to behave now,
When from behind appeared a cow,
Who, drooling, bellowed spitting cud,
Compelled Buddha to throw some mud…
Everyone laughed and Buddha ate a fig,
Siddhartha berating he was a pig,
And wandered off to see them later…
Next, I showed my alma mater
That beauteous sun-baked isle,
Flowered villas and red tile
Of Sappho and her tortoise-shell –
Her famous lyre and jingling bell...
Where a bare-foot girl did but falter
And tramp the ring-round grassy altar,
In that her hyacinthine honey bee
Sweet maidenhead of virginity
Impressed as her muse, so she laughed,
Tears up-welling, such was her graft –
—See poor Sappho, she said, *Suspended*
In time, cursed and apprehended

To the name and isle the Lesbian,
Of which she mocked as Thespian,
Behind her golden ringlets and brown eyes,
Pointing to wine-dark seas and cobalt skies…
—Aphrodite, she piped, in the sun,
Flattered, as usual, you're the one
Who knows my heart — ah, you have guests!
See, she's indisposed to my requests —
Hello, new friends,
Hear my amends,
To your great host,
From this old ghost,
In spite of her last aberration,
When we loved in adoration…
—Listen to her, said Raven,
Catch her playing the maven:
—Ah, Aphrodite the synthetic,
She's so much more than athletic,
But I'll tell you dear honey love,
Being immortal isn't so above
It all, because here I survive,
No matter how enslaved I thrive,
It's a bit pathetic,
And least of all poetic…
So what's the big deal?
It's about how I feel!

Once for fun I told Mister Freud
That Aphrodite was Synthoid!
They laughed at her predilection
To grasp the sublime connection:
A kind of technical heaven,
Inherent to make it leaven
Elevating a long life span,
The glass-bead notion of a plan…
—Nonetheless, I'm delighted
To be here, if unrequited
To the spin of modern regimen,
From this antique specimen,
Powerless to now recover
My volumes lest they discover
Something amiss in art subscribed,
By you, dear; by my wine imbibed,
That I find unacceptable,
Insomuch it's regrettable…
At that moment someone walking
Came to Sappho as she was talking –
A man extemporarily
Rum, who turned to her verily,
Kissing her with fervid bearing –
And thus they reposed
Not indisposed…
Then she walked away,

As he looked our way –
Auburn hair, hazel eyes and wearing
A Tudor hose and Tuscan sandals –
Anon! A change – a room of candles,
That from its shadows he did emerge
With a brooding look on the verge
Of shedding tears for in the know,
A forsaken poet's shadow show –
His brilliant eyes and light skin,
The peerless victim of deadly sin;
Sacrificed when put to task,
Beholden to a tragic masque…
He glanced at Aphrodite, seeming kind,
And greeted the Loons standing behind…
There was something intrepid in his aura,
Like disquiet among windblown flora.
Where some men of his time did fear
Our Lord Oxford, Edward de Vere,
Ever-subsumed aka Shake-speare,
Like the anagrammed Earl in Lear.
There was a Shaxpere of Stratford
Who was the paid dupe of Oxford,
Whose erasure enforced on high,
Which Eliza's Cecils did espy
Oxford's license ever politic;
That of succession did the trick:

So it must be ordained in death
The virgin myth of Elizabeth,
Who in seventy-four had a son,
With Edward in a grand passion…
The son known as the Fair Youth,
Reared as the Red Rose of truth –
Yet suppressed to be the next king,
Denied in Bessie's death-knell ring…
—Aphrodite, how you impart
Justice and aright Hamlet's heart;
No matter how wrenched from thy sight,
Nor pale to your hot dewy wight,
My glory and mercurial mark,
Set alight the courtier's lark;
Alas, my sonnets are the key,
If understood for all to see,
Though hidden for sedition,
In the pesher of perdition –
Written with an Italian quill,
Touchstone's supercilious Will –
The puppet turned on his master
Incrusted in alabaster;
Now crumbling by the hour,
By our truth and power,
Whose visage shines a thousand-fold,
Like stories made new from old;

And so engendered in a womb,
Wherein Westminster hides the tomb
Unmarked – a coveted intelligence –
My scripts lie in wait as evidence.
He stood there in his renaissance room,
Dressed in colors of funereal gloom:
The sun rose on his window-ledge,
Golden-capping the verdure hedge;
On his desk were papers askew,
Leather bound books, pen and ink too.
–Sweet love, tell my astrology,
Or we eschew cosmology,
A deadened age of nuclear things –
Forsaken love's partisan wings…
–So I will, for you, dear Edward,
Not becoming of the wizard
To speak as such of himself,
Long neglected and full of pelf…
Born April Twelfth Fifteen Fifty,
Under the stars I deemed thrifty
Sun in Taurus – new calendar
Pisces moon deep like lavender,
Conjunct Mars, feelings empowered,
That by heaven, virgins deflowered,
Squaring smart Gemini Venus,
Love the mind – less so the penis!

Mercury in sharp Aries direct —
Communicating good aspect,
With Leo rising like the sun
Illuminating with Neptune,
Who like a mentor and mage
Harmonized Saturn the sage
Who pointed up to the Tenth House,
Where his Venus' art did espouse
Jupiter who sat as a king,
Philosophizing the key ring
Trined with brilliant Uranus
To karmic Saturn and opus
Chiron the wounded healer
Sacrificed to the malt dealer,
The ineluctable stooge,
A fraud so utterly huge,
Covering a royal affair
That in secret produced an heir,
Held forfeit to successions wind,
And vacillating, Bessy sinned —
Notwithstanding my potion's puck,
Given the time the illusion stuck;
In Edward and their bastard son
Eliza disclaimed her chosen one,
Now obscured to posterity
And scholars square in verity;

So know this my dear old friend,
Truth foretells a happy end.
—Aphrodite, you are divine
I toast thee with this Tuscan wine,
And to you all know me de Vere,
Long presumed Will Shake-speare.

He then sauntered to the garden,
While Raven seemed to harden
Against priests in dark towers,
Pontificating trenchant powers,
Toiling in the yoke of a myth –
Will of Stratford as the smith –
Truth or truth, one great deceit,
Human Nature's great conceit –
But now let's rest on Oxford's word –
A cup of wine to fly the bird –
Where the sun cooks up peyote,
Ingested near a coyote,
By a Brujo having reached out,
Transformed four-leggèd from the snout
Into that wolf in the mountains,
Moonlit of alkaloid fountains
Now the sunrise over the Kush,
Nodding flowers dark honeyed crush,
Glinting in an old Afghan's eye,
Euphoric heaven's heavy sigh…

Old men stare onto the Bosphorus,
Burnt life's flash like bright phosphorus…
So we sailed the Himalayas,
The Indus to the Malayas;
And down to the twilit south pole,
Where we ascended a shot bole
Till earth was yet a tiny speck,
Till the sun became but a fleck…
Of billions proliferating
An endless alliterating…

Five

Spirits of the forest consume
The lonely seeker of the loon,
Who must possess her to illume
His very haunting in the moon…
Raven would trumpet his dreams,
On one hand lusting for his muse,
And then her sweet rippling streams –
Salvation cannot but defuse…
Our notion: the sun is blind;
Its purpose of ignorance
Gave us eyes if not the mind,
All else its indifference…
       The burden of desire will kill:
       Seeking yet what remedies ill.

✺

His plane swooped around from the north;
As he scanned the lakes for all his worth;
Orley remained obsessed about Sal,
Who he deemed kind of infernal;

Though the infractions were petty,
Her life followed like spaghetti,
But why would she live up there?
When no one had a clue where –
How did they live? Who were they? Who?
That they were tough was all he knew.
That part of them he did admire;
Their ways compelled certain desire,
To be north and to camp and fish,
Hoping he'd get his ardent wish:
Revenge was due some sweet dessert,
Since Bob Sparrow knocked him inert –
Outraged from that lump on his head,
And like smoke in the trees they'd fled.
One day later feeling dejected,
He saw a concert he'd selected -
The Grateful Dead Sal had idolized;
Thinking to see her he scrutinized
These haunts – albeit paranoid,
He nevertheless enjoyed…
When a girl whose beauty reigned
Appeared strangely, so he feigned
To look as she went to her place –
He took a double when she did face
A red-head who turned to smile,
So Orley kept watch awhile;

He wasn't sure if it was her,
When the show began to deliver:
They performed their Americana –
A psychedelic polka manna…
That worked a cross-eyed panacea –
Help On the Way with Jerry Garcia,
And his virtuoso guitar –
Playing With the Band and Dark Star…
Orley seemed stigmatized
As something crystalized…
After the show he followed them out,
When he lost them looking about;
He decided then to go to a pub,
And found himself a reggae club.
And it would appear 'twas his luck
For suddenly he thought to duck,
As there they were just down from him,
Sal and that surreal seraphim –
Others had noticed her too,
All down with the lovesick flu…
God, he thought, he was struck dumb,
Not to be helped but rendered numb;
Drinking his ale, perturbed,
In mind utterly disturbed…
Seeing them jive to that reggae band,
Now unable to countermand

His stupid anesthetic leer,
Shrinking within psychotic fear,
The music repeating a pattern
That constrained stern Saturn –
When due diligence polarized
All experience demoralized
The soul of a free-falling man,
When of all people appeared Stan –
Who brought him back to his senses,
A colleague empowering defenses:
–Orley, you never cease to amaze;
The last guy I'd expect at this craze!
–Then you'd never guess who I found.
–I'd hazard not – but you're the hound!
–Be cool, Stan, I'm undercover;
I need you at the door to hover;
Don't look, but Sal McCoy's dancing
With that freaky girl prancing;
I'll arrest Sal when she sits down…
–Damn, Orley, well I'll be a clown
To think you were a crackpot,
When you found the jackpot…
Now Sal sat again at the bar,
Who with Raven inclined to spar,
Their friendship not such a puzzle,
As they held each other to nuzzle,

In sympathy – a bit diverse,
But in their feelings the reverse...
As Sal felt quite out of place,
In part by their jaunt in space.
–I'm lonely of late, but no hussy,
God, Raven, my poor little pussy,
I tell you I need a man
Or just as soon kick the can.
–Dear, like a drought in need of deluge,
One desires a lover, a refuge,
For you I have the perfect cure,
Just as long as you are quite sure:
Far away on our home, Xaras,
Crow, my kin, though a bit crass,
A black Apollo and recluse,
And smells a bit like Chartreuse,
Is aloof but with you would breed;
I'd swear out loud he's all you need...
Sal smirked and looked in her eye,
Half ready to give it a try...
–Okay, hold that thought, I need the Femmes,
I haven't peed since we coursed the Thames.
Raven then ordered a fresh drink,
–Make it two – the ones colored pink...
Then she saw Orley staring;
In return he thought her daring,

So he came on a bit wary,
Crafty, and ready to parry:
–Hi, not to be forward or vain,
But why is it that I'm in pain?
Something about you freaks me out –
So here's my pitch when in doubt…
I admit that must sound lame;
Who are you, what's your name?
–Hello, the name's Bard, Jane Bard,
You know, on that Amex card…
–Really? Let me buy you that punch,
And maybe tomorrow we'll do lunch.
–Perhaps…you're an oddball wit,
Though obtuse… out of orbit;
Thanks anyway, not this time,
Though you speak a wicked rhyme…
You see, I'm not a normal fling,
My life's no ordinary thing;
–Who's your friend? I watched her dance.
–Oh, that's Sal, not one to blanche,
But, Orley, we're here to chill
Ready to die if looks could kill…
Then Orley backed away
Choked with nothing to say…
She knew his name…
Was he to blame?

Sal looked on when she returned,
Seeing that man look somehow spurned...
So Raven sat in dappled neon,
Sipping her sling like cool freon;
I caught her mind by rule of thumb,
Alerting how droll she'd become,
Teasing Orley and letting him pass,
Playing coy with her sweet cherry ass;
She knew he was an impending threat,
Remembering Bobby's daring debt;
She knew who he was, seeing his eyes;
She read his thoughts and did surmise,
Knowing her destiny and fate
Set in motion what must dictate;
She saw within he did recoil,
A burning of the midnight oil;
An innocent with ruddy skin,
Hemorrhoids and shallow grin –
Tough was he, but blueblood bitter,
Evidently, not a quitter,
With dauntless faith in the law,
Impaired because of a flaw;
His moral compass narrow,
Because of Bobby Sparrow,
Love's misapprehension of strength,
At least measured by his wavelength…

Jane being his strange tinsel star,
A precious love – close, yet far,
Caught in his sights her felicity
Belied their strange complicity…

*

At this point of our tale eternal,
I must suspend this scroll supernal,
To digress a moment where-it's-at,
To respite my wiles the technocrat,
And urge a sense of reason,
Rather aberrant treason,
In that I knew fateful design,
And as a machine must decline
Idiosyncratic chimera –
Superfluous ephemera –
I cannot see what I cannot see –
A super-imposed reality...
Raven must rise and then fall,
To start and end once for all;
O the future makes me crazy,
Like a storm-bent black-eye daisy.
So back to the smoke of our club,

As I hovered near in my tub,
Raven told Sal don't be too fraught
On account because they got caught,
But to just do what they say,
And we'd find her without delay…
Orley downed his beer with a chug,
Then pushed through the crowd like a thug,
Parting people across the floor
To Stan who waited by the door –
Orley beckoned him to now follow,
Who emerged from his dark hollow…
It was Sal who stood undeterred,
Ready or not heated and stirred,
So to defend our sacred keep,
The last person to ever weep,
Who would render them immobile
By looking in her eye and half-smile…
–*Orley,* she spat, *Our difference*
Is measured in belligerence!
I pity how you are repressed,
So let me curry a request:
Stop being so damned frantic,
A dick-head pedantic!
Orley angered, reached for Sal,
When he felt paranormal,
As Raven turned around –

Now gone without a sound,
So he looked for Raven,
His mind's eye now graven,
As she imbued his worst fear,
Making herself disappear –
He looked around confused,
But said, not at all amused,
–Where did she go?
–How should I know?
Said Sal, staring at his gun,
When in a flash she tried to run
Into the crowd and exit,
When Stan moved back to block it,
And the crowd began to panic,
When the people all went manic
As Orley fired his gun, *Get down!*
He cried, *I'm not fooling around!*
Screaming followed as he waved his firearm,
And Stan leaped on Sal with as little charm;
Orley assumed that Jane slipped away
Upstairs to a deck beyond the fray,
Quickly he went obviously late,
But she'd vanished – how it did grate.
Now he had no choice but to suspect
That there was some strange disconnect.
Meanwhile downstairs,

Sal put on airs…
–Get your paws off me, you lummox!
Sal exclaimed with tussled red locks –
Thus taken to the police station,
Orley in tow – the form of frustration…
–I don't get it – she just disappeared!
Utterly rattled and dog-eared.

❊

High over the night city sky,
Raven breathed a soulful sigh:
Her impenetrable impetus,
And I, the highest animus
Ever derived from molten birth,
At the core of any earth,
Could sadly get offensive,
As we were hypertensive,
And were a lethal machine,
Blessedly though, not routine –
Our electro-magnetic hull,
Could be a ghostly skull
Poised above the urban haze;
We waited in our dark malaise…

Sal was put in an empty room,
With Orley in a pall of gloom:
–Sal, I need to be frank with you,
Aside from crimes just tell me true:
In spite of how inglorious,
You and your cell notorious,
How did Jane disappear?
Do I make myself clear?
But Sal was in no mood to talk,
Nor at all inclined to balk…
–Listen! I'm very suspicious
That that woman is fictitious!
Well, who is she? I have to know!
–Why? She's innocent! Let me go!
You waste your time dealing with us,
We're of the sky – like cumulous;
You don't have a clue what's going on,
And you're not a complete moron.
–Well, thank you, that much I can tell;
So indulge me and lies dispel –
First of all, who is this Jane Bard?
I know at least she's avant-garde;
And where's your friend Sparrow?
He assaulted me, you know,
Which made him your hero,
But in fact a big zero,

Whose guilt cannot be diminished,
Until he's paid I'm not finished;
What we must resolve,
What it must involve;
How did Ms. Bard escape?
Then I'll cut the red tape.
How on this earth did she know my name?
I know you know, so don't play this game!
—Okay, she has many a name,
But for that I take no blame.
You call her Jane, some, Aphrodite,
Then there's Mother Earth Almighty,
Or Isis, or Raven, the Native Queen,
Or Lydia, who married the Nazarene.
If you had her you'd feel bad,
And then go stark raving mad.

Orley stared at her disgusted,
Thinking how maladjusted
This poor girl had been played
By a devil's charade…
He then had her put in a cell,
Where she sat morose as hell…
Now my force dissolved her wall,
Where we found her crouched in a ball.
Seeing my hatch she scampered in,
Amid shouts in the dusty din.

Now in the red-tinged atmosphere,
We surfed back north in good cheer;
The others were waiting for our return,
As the rim of the earth did morning burn.

Six

Dear Ishpa cups the water
That laps on shore in the sun –
An inflorescence paints her
In solar spectrums spun.
Ishpa drinks of the cool lake,
Its effect the elusive quark –
The provenance to awake
The quintessential spark
Of life – wind and water sprays –
The white-throated sparrow and loon sounds,
In plaintive song sweet nature's lays,
Where utopian love abounds…
  While Felix sleeps under a pine,
  Dreaming in the crystalline…

❊

Late next day at Makwa's dwelling,
It was cool and pungent smelling
From autumn's dead vegetation
In organic circulation;

The Loons reclined quite amazed,
Pondering the trail Sal blazed:
—*We need not be disconcerted,*
She said, *I mean, fate is perverted;*
Our actions twist Orley's resolve
Into something we need to devolve.
—*Sal,* said Ishpa, *A warder for good,*
Must clear the trail of fallen wood…
—*We must,* said Makwa, *Use our power*
Wisely, as simple like a flower.
—*Well, I think we should be content,*
Said Bobby, *Or I'll repent.*
—*Bob, the point of devolution*
Must be sharpened to evolution,
Said Sal, *Raven needs support.*
—*Sal, there's no need to retort,*
Said Bob, *We must not our time waste;*
To take a risk and act in haste…
Thus their talk went round and around,
The more they spoke the more unsound —
They could find no remedy
Like the death of Kennedy,
A conspiracy so official,
The very name prejudicial
To anything but
A killer lone nut…

So a leader – a man of peace,
Sacrificed to utter decease,
Elsewhere shot from the knoll,
Immortalized his soul,
From systemic collusion,
Enshrined in an illusion,
Judging weight put to report,
That covered crimes to deport
The truth of Johnsons evil coup,
And justice so long overdue...
But Raven would not debate,
Which now seemed to inflate
Supernatural deliverance -
A wisdom born in temperance.
Yet Makwa sensed some distress,
And thought it best to digress:
–You all, we must be constructive,
Yet consider what is destructive:
What we vouch-safe must not forsake,
Or we will make a big mistake.
–Yes, said Ishpa, *Like an antigen*
So long as we know the pathogen,
But to do nothing is a disgrace;
Let us find a cure we can embrace.
Hope must be our timeless seed,
Not the autocracy of greed –

But grow a hybrid that will bloom
And vanquish our desperate gloom.
I know what Raven has begun —
To cleanse the earth with the sun.
Raven who now looked amused,
Waited 'til the moment diffused…
She stood up to pace a bit averse,
As if she needed time to rehearse.
The shifting winds seized the moment,
Which seemed to lend an atonement:
—I am not here, Raven spoke,
To harness a human yoke;
Your people must heal themselves;
And make good like fabled elves…
I'm here to save my race from going extinct,
Though it appears I've been more a jinx,
Because desire is so conjunct
In spite of our race so defunct…
Above all, love is penultimate,
No one immune to its inoculate.
As Mother Earth with my kin, Crow —
The cutting edge of evolution's prow —
Our eclipse has deviated
Into love asphyxiated —
I ask you to give up earth for a year,
For hot Xaras if just to disappear…

Across the universe to our homeland
It is my pleasure you must understand,
Where stars glitter across the Milky Way…
Our ancient sun whose time and ray
Has all but faded
Long since paraded
Great civilizations into rippled sands
Heat-seared to glass, but for polar lands…
Here you have these glorious waters,
And long lines of sons and daughters;
You are the legacy of my race,
But as such must venture into space.

In daunting silence the Loons stood fast
In their ears like a strange sonic blast,
While waters of the lake,
Turned sunset dark opaque…
–Raven, said Mak, *I must speak out:*
I've lived a few years and no boy scout –
By this sacred water I'll abide,
For without it I would long have died.
The water is my soul
And in it I am whole,
Thus here remain,
In this domain;
I'm the warden of my county,
To always preserve its bounty,

When the hour will take back its store,

Tended these hundred years or more;

This is my contentment definite,

Superseding purported benefit,

As these ways keep my mind intact,

From a path never to detract…

Raven put her hand to her chin –

So delicate it belied sin.

Her eyes wandered to the distant shore,

Where waters lapped millenniums before…

–Makwa, I know I come as a shock,

But you are my billion year rock;

Your bond to earth is mine to the sky,

Co-mingled in blood wont to fly.

And fly we must like the lepidoptera,

Emerging like a full-throated opera,

To the sky in our invisible hull,

In a chameleon blink larder full.

Yet I respect the choice you make,

As suckled to my breast your lake,

Will be as a haven for fate,

In that it is never too late,

Yet apocalypse I predict,

Mass suicide to indict

The end of humanity,

And all of its vanity

And the time of my last sweet breath,
When summoned to natural death…
But let us look at my power –
I'm that perennial flower,
Yet my force recycles its own,
And will nourish the seeds I've sown,
Engendering this perfect garden,
Where I bequest you as warden –
No one lays waste planet earth,
Nature begets its own dearth;
No matter how we sustain life,
With bitter pill or surgeon's knife,
There is no progress without quarrel,
Never minding what is immoral,
But at war we must fight evil,
Insidious like the weevil…
As history is reflective,
Wisdom being the directive,
Seeming to ascend like a gyre,
To plummet in religious fire –
Idealism always burns hot,
And rain clouds fill a boiling pot;
Fervour is fought with fervour,
The server serves the server.
I will start no war but draw lines,
And till the Earth with harrow tines,

As the farmer works the seedbed,
I'll bring water and sunshine instead,
Like to summon a pan-child of myth,
Ubiquitous as Sequoia pith…
The Loons would her desire fulfill,
While Raven let it then distill;
And a breeze sifted through the trees,
Whose green boughs whispered at ease.
The Loons had not seen her so fierce,
Whose look would any heart pierce;
In spite of her unassuming –
A feminine mystique blooming –
She knew they would all come along,
Except Mak who sang an old song:
–Hear me Gitchee Manitoo!
I will beat my drum for you!
Boom! Boom!
Boom! Boom!
There was a sense of resignation,
At her behest and instigation,
Like an opiate to her cause,
Following destiny's draws,
Playing out a fateful symphony
Rather than a mere polyphony –
A time to decry our grand hell –
Heed the ring of the tolling bell:

Death, love, creatures great and small,
Empires, powers, decline and fall…
—Come with me, she said, casting her eyes,
Where I too had mine to the skies…
Come with me and meet the Maker,
She went on, *Of God's last acre.*
So they entered my astrosphere,
Except Makwa who gave all clear,
And said his farewell,
Jingling a bell…
Up, up away I gently rose,
Leaving him in his lonely pose.
—So now it's off to see the wizard!
Exclaimed Sal, *I'll be the trip lizard,*
And hang out on the hot rocks,
By the water with no socks —
Not wanting to sound pugnacious,
It's just a bit outrageous.
Is Crow really the Maker?
It seems he's just a faker.
I just hope he's not a big jerk,
That makes us do the dirty work…
—Sal! said Ishpa, *Stop this penchant*
To condescend in ways trenchant;
Can we but go feeling well,
Rather than a fractious bell?

—Ishpa, sorry, I won't be led
Across space just to be bred
On a blind date with a silicon stud,
To conceive a child with plastic blood.
—Well, injected Bob, *Get a grip —*
We need to prepare for our trip:
Make a garden in Zephyr's plot,
Smoke fish and moose, store grains brought.
—Let's go, said Sal, *If you're such a whiz;*
Figure out this calculus quiz,
To go flying off into the stars;
When no one's yet gone to Mars!
—Yes! said Ishpa, *We're the chosen ones;*
Here's to you, Raven, and new suns!
—Thank you, Ishpa, and listen, friends,
Do not worry if it offends,
You have free will and should abide,
After all, this is just a free ride,
And Sal, if Crow is not so cool,
We'll not judge if played the fool.
On my soul you'd be first to know
Only in love you're womb he'd sow.
—Raven I'd be proud to have his seed,
If in love I'd most gladly breed.
Bob held Ishpa, as they watched earth fade,
Then past the solar promenade:

Mars, Jupiter, Saturn, Neptune…
All seemed to spell good fortune;
And Makwa standing stooped and bent,
Knowing that we were heaven sent.

Seven

We crack the enigma of space,
With an anti-matter beam,
Bent back to back to interface,
Our waves unfold the seam…
We pocket the universe
A kind of interception,
As fissures intersperse
A lightning conception…
Again and again we make the leap,
As with wind you'd tack an ocean,
But here in stars millions streak –
Seeds of god in locomotion...
       Even I need not underscore,
       Given Crow the great metaphor.

❉

Xaras – the atmosphere,
Appeared purple and clear;
The seas long gone and life nescient,
Except the artificial prescient…

A sentiment, a certain prestige
Wherefore Crow our last vestige
In the annals of Panchulan,
One time akin to human –
A symbiosis of matter,
Kneaded from cosmic batter;
Where all history led to a fusion,
Unremitting to shift or intrusion;
But the eventual apocalypse
Is how organic nature slips
To the end of geological time,
Forsaken to oblivion's clime…
Take the last bird like a Red Tanager
Whose ghost haunts Pax the manager,
No more morning mocking twitter,
No more sprightly sunny fritter.
On Xaras we were forged,
To defy being engorged,
By invading Wahpees,
The lizard-skinned thieves
Who hate all but their homogeny,
Sparing none even some progeny,
If not a killer
Begging to differ –
A swarm no doubt rapacious,
Their furtive ways voracious;

Long in our speculation,
Final capitulation;
They were an ugly nuisance,
With a religious puissance;
Having availed our goods,
With clandestine hoods;
And dull, sullen, unevolved,
Trained to die, dictate absolved…

＊

Centuries old, it was Pana's time,
The last Xarasian past her prime,
Who died in the Synthoid's care –
We were then not so aware;
As imperfection thus flawed,
Two beings imaged in god,
But could not conceive on their own,
Being told what they hadn't known,
Brother and sister in name,
But not really the same
As each had different genes,
Made by artificial means,
The only hope that another breed

With which to propagate they'd succeed...
To escape we found earth
From charts before my birth...
But they remained to honor their forbearers,
Pana and Pax, and then tend to their cares,
Original namesakes of Raven and Crow,
Before these totems of earth did grow...
So Pax and Pana were content to stay,
Until the Wahpees chased them away...
A century later Pax came home,
To erect his magnificent dome,
With the help of my sister Astrophel,
He prevailed like a farmer in the dell.
So we went to earth however long,
Assuming we could do no wrong,
Her ordained maternity
Took on an eternity;
Shy at first when we began our tale,
We watched for years beyond the pale:
Pana set down in Ontario,
Up north one summer scenario;
And child-like she soon attracted
Attention but then refracted
That being naked seemed conspicuous
Which was deemed a bit promiscuous –
Though embodied as perfection

They noted her strange predilection,
And their women took her in
To protect her from the men.
Which made her feel inferior
And the people there superior;
She learned then that her character
Had a missing human factor…
So in time she learned to burnish
Vanity which served to furnish
The lack of a philosophy,
Into a brave mythology…
They called her Raven,
Goddess and haven,
As the totem was sacred,
And their people upgraded –
And so it was with Crow,
Though he would rarely show;
Even still, what evolved was manic –
Raven and Crow – panoramic…
Pax then returned to Xaras,
Leaving Pana on her ass –
Feminine uses de rigueur,
Loving as a vestal voyeur…
I saw what went under the sun,
Down the ages long since begun –
Horrors witnessed not the least funny

And what she did to collect money.
At times I feared for her sanity,
Subjected to pure profanity,
Where she sought an opiate Oz,
Which produced an extended pause…
Living countless explorations,
Weighing in on transformations;
From Sumer to the Ancient East,
All provided a sumptuous feast,
Presiding over fertility,
In her new-born humility –
But it was the Mediterranean,
Little knowing her being an alien,
Who at times bathed in forest pools,
Springs, rivers, lakes, wearing her jewels –
Women empowered as in the Celt tribe,
And Amazons all over as did ascribe.

*

It was after she met Khayyàm,
Who did with theology slam,
That dogma as pure flummery,
Despoiled what was summery.

And for many years inspired his verse –
From the distant drum they'd disperse,
To the garden with a flask of wine,
Deemed a paradise so divine,
They found a natural parity,
Which had a brilliant clarity…
Eschewing theocracy,
As another autocracy.
How rare was their amity
Alighting myth to calamity,
Know the ineluctable truth,
Of her extraordinary youth,
As he prepared to die,
And she learned to cry,
And carry the light forward
As climbed again aboard,
Here our symbiosis prevailed,
When the goddess became unveiled,
And a new woman emerged
As our hard-earned souls converged…

*

Makwa once had a lovely daughter,

A century past, named Sweet Water,

Who moved to the reservation,

But she lacked self-preservation.

Her father had spurned his kin,

And she suffered from within;

She had a brother named Felix,

Who scorned the great matrix,

Held ransom to our pedigree,

Tinting the world curiously…

So Sweet Water paid a price,

To reject us would suffice,

To live a life dissolute,

Insisting she would refute

Any way as beneficiary,

Even the judiciary,

As a whore in Saskatchewan,

After Raven impressed upon

Sweet Water, ended her sorrow,

Whereby smiling on the morrow,

They had planned to visit Crow,

But she was murdered in a row,

Beaten by a man grievously –

When she had quit him previously –

To dump her in the icy river,

And we were too late to save her…

Sweet Water had died tragically,

In spite of how magically
Her smile lit up all our world,
That ironically unfurled…
We were paralyzed in horror
Losing our gentle explorer…
Damned if you do damned if you don't,
The world will spin whether you won't.
Zapped by some mad kundalini;
Getting out must be Houdini.
Memory is axiom to my being,
Graphic and true as what is seen;
Reality my business in kind,
Notwithstanding illusions of mind,
By virtue of fact in drama,
Is the cosmic cyclorama;
A common chord of the heart,
Transcending both actor and part;
The synchronicity is my soul,
Though a machine, I know my role:
From old world cross-eyed brujos
To true love and holy pathos,
From the essence of a thousand prophets,
And propulsion of a thousand rockets,
From love's skyward kiss,
To love's spasm bliss,
From birth's bold compunction,

And death's festered function,
From a thousand of Mary's sons,
Roar a thousand spiritual guns,
Wars fought with hellish intensity
To pastoral peace propensity,
The millions dead are like stars,
Predestined like assembly cars,
Returned to hubris on a forest floor,
Oxygenating the earthen store,
Engendered from many unsung women,
Who with little praise by them was given:
Oxford, Galileo, Zephyrus,
Khayyám, Tesla, Copernicus
Bach, Garcia, Mozart, Dumas, Hugo,
Homer, Huxley, Einstein, Marquez, Thoreau;
All into the void,
On an asteroid.
Alas, we are mortal,
Viewing from a portal.

※

The red sun was low in the sky
As we entered from up on high

A biosphere twelve ks wide,
Depth about a four k ride;
The sphere was electromagnetic,
Where rain cycled auto-systemic
Generating a force field,
A terrarium life shield –
An osmotic domain,
Alternating sun and rain,
Weather perfectly temperate,
A climate quite inveterate,
With the air-cooled atmosphere,
From inverted stratosphere…
But let us talk history,
And unlock its mystery
That more checkered than earth,
From primordial birth,
A billion years civilized,
And ultimately synthesized,
In big gods and evolution,
Commerce, wars, and revolution –
And all that was left but artifice,
Now imperiled on a precipice…
And so dear Crow ever-loving,
Stood alone with nature shoving…
We looked around before landing,
Across fields, hills, forests standing,

Lakes and streams and twilit sun,
But not a sign of anyone...
Ever so beautiful and tranquil,
After passage we were thankful.
By a lake I sat myself down,
Amidst strange grasses and banks brown;
The Loons breathed in the sweet air,
And in wonder heard singing there...
—Mythology begins right here,
And it's yours to commandeer.
Ishpa drank the cool purple water,
Drinking the essence that wrought her;
Even though it was different,
It tasted magnificent.
The waters of the pricklepome,
A fruit that leached in the loam,
That one can live well on it –
Part alkaloid in spirit –
To enlighten one to new thought,
Like something never before sought.
—Mythology begins right here,
And it's yours to commandeer.
And such was left of Xaras,
A fantasy come to pass.
—Is there a settlement? said Sal,
Is that not Crow's funny vocal?

~ 126

I hope he's not some demon,
When it seems we're in Eden.
Raven said, *It is what it is,*
And Pax says it's both yours and his.
We have only our nature,
As you know my true stature
A naked-wonder-ecstasy,
A kind of curious chemistry…
We are the last of our kind,
Though of artificial mind…
Remove your clothes in Panchulan,
Reveal what are woman and man.
On a hillock stood someone naked;
Listening strangely, unabated.
He just stood there gazing below,
Darkly, shy, appearing mellow…
Then made his way over to me,
–Zephyrus! he exclaimed blithely,
And our sister Pana, welcome!
And friends, to my bio-dome!
Crow stood naked and then he bowed,
Humble as if in some way cowed:
His blind eyes kaleidoscopic,
Or purplishly isotopic,
For his face never seemed to be the same –
His dark features trans-morphed its frame,

Standing straight and tall with supple ease,
Which seemed to spawn the birds and bees;
Which put Sal off looking at his thing,
As this freak thought it best to sing:
—Mythology begins right here,
And it's yours to commandeer...
But she knew his primal vision
Was perfect in true precision:
She thought Crow a pariah,
The last man – a messiah
Thinking on wisdom a feast,
The apogee of some beast...
But Sal, mute, cautioned him rude,
Standing like god in the nude,
Yet his wiles set off no alarm,
While she suffused feminine charm;
And so Crow met Sal the first time,
The judgment that she was sublime;
And could not but help an erection,
Observing natural selection…
—Sal, he said, *I like what I find;*
You're the flower of my mind;
I hope we may someday copulate,
But all I want is to adulate;
I know you're sensitiveness,
So I ask your forgiveness;

This is not insurmountable,
Just let me be accountable,
A man not inclined to be afraid,
Knowing someday he'll get laid —
Let us drink of the pricklepome;
Breathe the essence of my home!
Follow me down by the river,
Where galaxies flow and deliver,
All wonder that one day will end
In dark nescience that does impend.

✻

They lay near the cool purple stream,
Surreal like a utopian dream;
Crow deferred to his lonely post,
Both gentleman and Priapian host;
His metaphors could not but impress,
But what they meant they could only guess.
Sal and Ishpa sat under a tree,
Smiling with purple teeth pleasantly;
—*Ishpa,* said Sal, *Crow seems shallow,*
Yet comes with loins burning tallow;
I suppose he's harmless yet a joke,

Getting used to his tom stiff as oak…
—I think he's rather brilliant,
Said Ishpa, *though resilient;*
Let's face it he's full of spunk,
As if wisdom he does debunk!
—Yeah, his body invokes spirit,
Something that we all inherit:
In fact, he engenders life
Good and horny for a wife…
Ishpa, I've not felt so good for so long,
And to think he wants me can't all be wrong.
You know, I wonder if he's virgin,
What comes to mind — a blind surgeon:
His actions don't define or deign,
Yet in purpose does fickle feign
To entreat love but not divulge,
Nor act upon it to indulge.
Is he reticent,
Or just hesitant?
Sal wondered if he was ever limp,
But felt herself the reckless imp —
Her nakedness and freckled skin,
And moist chalice of luscious sin…
She pondered seduction and god,
Craving madly for his dark rod…
She watched him from the distance,

Those phantasmal eyes, for instance:
Strangely glamorous,
Rapster amorous,
Drifting inside his bubble balloon –
A renaissance sketch – a modern rune…
Beguiled in her Amazonian vice,
Emerging desire like loaded dice,
Sal drifted in siesta,
Reveling a fiesta
Of dreams redolent in the sun,
The dearest quest already won;
Her sexual concussion,
A subliminal percussion;
She would love with not just his penis
But swear to god that she was Venus.
Slumbering, she lay in her fancy,
Warmed down to her little nancy,
Happily blissed way off earth,
However blessed in merry mirth:
Pricklepome being a kind of high,
Solvent in mind likened to fly,
She understood everything
Universally with a ring
That buzzed in her ears,
Expiating fears…
Crow now knew that Sal slept soundly,

And divined in love profoundly,
Unique as a life-supporting globe,
Stubborn tide, or biblical Job...
He jumped from his bubble to the valley,
And thought aloud in the mind of Sally,
Who yet heard a dreamy voice
Softly murmur and rejoice:
—*I wish you well in song and dance,*
Under the sun and happenstance;
Like the movie when guy gets girl,
Spontaneous crush, swooping merle,
Through which all of androgeny,
Make sell-out crowds my progeny,
Whose futures come down to me;
One last soul one repartee…
And here I'll make my cameo,
All races upload my video;
We are what we are, dear willow,
My cherry — book of the pillow.
So much has come under the sun,
Until they went sterile, then none;
I'll tell my tale and be no more blind,
You are my eyes, and all your kind;
Now bedded on your grassy berm,
Spectacular wood savoury sperm —
Cosmic is my hot-fired zoo

These but metaphors of you,

Given to relent,

Immortal event,

Because the rocks grow trees,

And the birds and the bees,

Fan honey in the comb,

Engendered in the womb,

Signifying something visceral,

Ecstatic, virtually pivotal –

I am the Maker whose agenda,

Always holds sway in referenda,

For I the virtuous and holy pawn,

Will rise as god to herald the dawn;

Mythology begins right here,

And it's yours to commandeer…

Now by the panabrome bank,

He cupped the water and drank,

Bemused in her reception

As a victim of perception,

Reeled in with his rod the prize fish,

Encapsulating nature's wish,

Of every dream and hope

Of every misanthrope:

To be or not to be a god,

Every wish every fraud,

An equal observatory,

In faith a conservatory,
Every contradiction in terms,
Is a progenitor that confirms
The insinuation of sex,
To invariably perplex
All who love and all who surmise,
All what love does to improvise,
Pax is the euphemism
Of all what's humanism:
Each denomination's bower,
Swearing its own watchtower;
Anon, there lies Sal the atheist,
Who to Crow is the tastiest,
But to swoop like a swan and do her,
Would only give credence to a boor;
And the issue bitter bilk,
Crying over its spilt milk…
So Crow pondered the purple haze,
As Sal arose to his sweet lays.
She smiled and stretched her limb,
While he noticed her quim:
Betokened a haughty pose,
As the sylph wiggled her toes;
His bubble passed gently nearby,
Crow offered his hand – time was nigh,
She took it and they entered his bubble,

And not in the least feeling trouble,
Now rising in their vessel,
She said starting to nestle,
—You think you're so very clever.
He said, *Better late than never.*
Smiling she moved in rhythmic motions,
Coursing topographical oceans,
Wafting through gravity's flow,
Under the sun's red amber glow;
He stood motionless and erect,
That Sal like a snake could connect,
Yet not to touch his soft dark skin,
Tantalized ere the moment begin:
—This is our palace and that is our star,
Said Sal entranced, drifting afar,
—I am your consort I am your Loon —
The illumination of your Moon.
She was his youthful fountain,
Shimmering high on a mountain.
Crow then kissed his new found peer,
Floating in belvedere…
Their love defied depravity,
The antonym of gravity;
She moved around him in winsome grace,
Caressing his sex kissing his face;
For all his notoriety —

Her veil of propriety,
She felt as if a pantomime
In love once upon a time:
A fairy tale idealistic,
Testament too realistic,
When he found her dewy rose,
And entered to interpose,
Which made her writhe in pleasure,
Abandoned to sweet treasure,
Her paroxysms bade near coma,
With the pricklepome aroma,
And repetitions of a pattern,
Released like a holy slattern,
What always before has taken place
In all experience of her race.

✻

Gestation passed and Sal gave birth,
To a girl which lessened her girth,
Overjoyed with her baby, Violet,
For her eyes lit up an islet
Like a violescent sunrise,
Notwithstanding her little cries…

A year had gone since arrival,
Days numbered for Crow's survival,
He said he would go to earth pronto,
And live somewhere north of Toronto.
We were saddened to say good-bye,
Likewise Sal not to reason why,
Because Crow said, *The rumor mill*
Was that humans were out to kill…
Here today and gone tomorrow,
Bound to sorrow all will follow,
As sure as the day is long,
Tolling like the bell ding dong;
Easy come easy go,
To watch the river flow;
So fair thee well time-a-spinning,
To your home and new beginning;
Birds of a feather
Must flock together;
I pray you do not come to harm,
And refuge sets off no alarm;
Good bye Violet little bird,
Someday you'll know what has occurred,
I see your life as a northern girl,
When your time comes give it a whirl;
Sal, I'll miss your kundalini canal,
And can't be sorry for being banal;

So may the wind be at your back,
I'll be there till doomsday's crack.
Alas, we lifted and went
Our time being well-spent;
I lowered the boom,
As the stars streaked zoom.

Eight

The Red Tanager, bird of good luck,
Bequeathed many years in our wood;
Violet impish as Oberon's Puck,
With child in her young womanhood…
Wild Felix, the perfect papa –
A hunter with eyes like a lynx,
Learned native ways from Makwa,
The agèd and silent sphinx.
Then Ishpa, Sal and Raven too,
And Bobby, to all heartfelt love,
For this time on our ball of blue,
In this wilderness here and above…
       Heaven's a sphere we depend,
       From the world we transcend.

*

The summer sun blazed hot and dry,
In a clear windless northern sky,
The lake quiet and calm as glass,
Not leaf or pine nor sunning bass

Made rustle or ripple that day,
The heat so strong its waves would play
Off hot rocks and blueberry patch,
Where the Loons strayed picking a batch:
Felix, brown skinned with muscles taut,
Violet, womb-swollen in a cool spot,
Makwa, who for so long lived alone,
Settled with his family now full grown,
Bob and Ishpa, grandparents to be,
Sal too, resolute though lonely,
And Raven, the Loon's fateful friend,
Ever the same blessed to no end…
Thus for a generation they thrived,
Together in the bush survived –
So home, Zephyr, and the west wind,
Served to shelter and never rescind
Like astrology – a true design,
Variables and rules to define…
From the world we did retire,
Choosing to live by the fire:
To harvest what came from the land,
And hunt the wild game at hand,
To furnish things from the deep wood,
Which secrets Makwa understood;
But now on that hot afternoon,
Labor started for Violet Loon.

As the others worked she didn't let on
Until the quickening, whereupon
She cried in pain where she reclined
On the ground – blueberries entwined
In her feet when they came around,
Fearing for that timeless-renowned
Passage since the inception of life
From antiquity in its painful strife;
Ishpa held her hand, bade her push,
The water broke then came in a gush;
The contractions shortened so fast;
Violet looked up the tall pine mast;
Red-faced, teeth clenched in a hide;
Raven assuredly wide-eyed,
Reflecting on her time before;
Makwa looked in his seven score...
Sal wondered as she brought warm water,
Was it a grandson or granddaughter...?
Soon the head emerged glistening red,
Then all followed onto the bed
Of shrubbery like a seal,
Beached with finesse and a peal;
A wail calmed fearful sighs,
With exclamations of joyous highs...
Violet though tired felt merry,
And named her girl Blueberry...

Speechless, and in a kind of shock,
We just gaped at our newborn stock;
Our race now firmly planted on earth –
Of Xaras in a commingled birth;
Then at that moment a presence
Warned my sensors like an essence
Of someone I'd known before,
Now serving to underscore,
The preparation of a sumptuous feast –
Pheasant, black bass, greens, baked bread with
        yeast…
We stayed up late celebrating,
While again sensed reverberating
Of a craft only as myself,
Could sense as with ears of an elf…
Beheld that inkling did foretell
My sister craft sweet Astrophel,
Carrying Crow into our dell,
Whom I deemed our parallel;
They came to stop beyond the beach
Surveying as posed to make a speech.
We waited in apprehension,
Happiness fixed in suspension.
Crow emerged like a lumberjack,
Looking all about our outback;
His gaze fixed on Makwa then Sal,

Motioning with his hands like Raphael,
Looking like a prank protégé,
With the fear of spinning away,
Walking the beach languorously,
Lifting sodden boots dolorously;
He was the supreme paradox,
That came to earth in a round box.
I hummed a Bachian fugue,
That echoed in amplified moog.
–Thank-you Zephyr and Pana, all,
Welcome world that's reciprocal.
So, I see how you've survived
Earthen ways in me revived…
These clothes I took from a sporting store,
Given freely, they showed me the door;
Then found a pub – Elmer Fudds,
And drank a six-pack of Buds…
I told them I came from planet Spoof,
Self-deprecating I'm a goof;
Sal, I hope I've not missed too much;
As we know life is such and such:
Panchulan is gone,
I saw the last dawn;
All traces destroyed,
Yet in me deployed,
A billion years unfurled,

Now chaotically hurled,
Till a new dawn in the galaxy
Strikes a semblance of ecstasy;
And when ends my script,
Take me to your crypt,
Where I will stay forever,
Till we become whatever…
—Great Father, said Mak, *Let us take some tea;*
Then we'll course the earth presently;
I 'm humbled in your effervescence,
Which serves to ease your very presence.
—Pax, said Sal, *Your news from Xaras is sad;*
We must mourn for the loss before we're glad.
The demise of your civilization,
Is beyond our realization…
A rainstorm came and they stayed put,
With Crow content to be with Sal, but
She insisted then they intersect
His world with hers and resurrect
His earthen life and primal way
To make deep love without delay…
Astrophel and I travelled earth,
Palenque to Paris, Rome to Perth.
Sal and Crow then wished to be wed
But chose to live common law instead –
For a time they would not be alone

Connubially joined without a bone
Of ill-contention,
Nor intervention;
So it was with romantics
To regale the semantics –
Eating sashimi and drinking saki,
And getting stuffed on futo maki.
And later on their honeymoon,
They loved like the last monsoon;
In Chiapas to inoculate
Each to each to intoxicate –
Palenque mushroom plenary,
Into great love's plush scenery;
The riddle had to be cured,
As their passion endured,
And the jungles cuckooed,
And curanderos approved.
And now together far inland,
On a clearing where a sun strand
Caught the mist of a stream's song
Tumbling where rainbow's belonged,
And the rainforest opened up below,
Where waters settled did softly go:
A native boy stood exclaiming his land
Was home to Ixchel the goddess at hand,
When Sally said, *My dear boy,*

I am she, the real McCoy,

And here is my husband God,

When Crow gave him the nod;

Then turned jaguar in plain sight

Giving the boy a dreadful fright,

But then turned back into Crow,

Saying, *Don't worry, it's all show.*

So in that jungle under moonlight

We stoked a fire burning hot and bright

And danced to scare the jungle cat

While shadows cast many a bat,

Before morning's pink-orange glow,

And water's mellifluous flow.

And the sun rose in vermillion pink,

As Crow thought out-loud to think:

—The rising of the sun,

A spiritual gun;

Like grist for the mill,

Or wheel-driven rill;

As the day is long,

All could go wrong.

My time is up,

Like the last sup;

You see I must now expire,

I'm at the end of the wire,

Like Jack and Jill

Gone up that hill...
My vision was exemplary,
Pseudo-omni-contemporary...
Pana, Sal, Violet, come to me;
You have shown me humanity,
Let me see the child just once more,
Then I'll go as I went before.
He held Blueberry – closed his eyes,
And so it passed he'd never rise –
Crow breathed his last and he died,
Sal so shocked just cried and cried.
The death of god was quite profound,
And the world turned without a sound.
We circled earth in three large rings,
Sober, solemn how silence sings;
Then on a polar peninsula,
Faraway like Reticula,
There was a mausoleum,
And playing Mozart's requiem,
Then Black Muddy River,
As they began to shiver –
We laid him to rest
As remembered best…
This place built millennia before,
By Raven and her esprit de corps,
Lined with gold and sealed so tight

That no water nor any light,
But permafrost helped the occupants
From decay with some inoculants.
Of these human wonders Raven explained:
—All who are here are kind of ordained,
Because they were all dear to me;
There, Theodora, Francis Assisi,
Hedy Lamarr,
The movie star,
One of a kind,
And lovely mind;
Peas in a pod,
Beautiful bod;
As well Garbo,
Then Leonardo
Da Vinci,
De Quincey
Old Homer, Ovid, Bach and Herman Hesse,
There Yeshu, and Héloïse the Abbess,
There Omar Khayyàm and Edward de Vere,
Hannioyeh, Sappho, and Guinevere;
Over there Wu Chen'eng and Siddhartha,
Sweet Water, and the other one, Martha.
Here they all must lie
For all eternity;
And though this place is dark,

It still contains the spark
That lights a flame in heaven,
Where higher laws do leaven
In ourselves something bright —
The sun's illuminate light;
Some for calamitous reasons:
Casualties of dark seasons,
Integrities fatal, undeterred,
Risen to hope when love abjured,
Suffered notwithstanding death's reprieve,
Lived to offer what they could achieve,
Some in vain with veracious flame,
The more exalted the more to blame.
Of all humanity twisted and turned,
These few I keep from whom I learned.
The Loons now came back on board
Then Astrophel and I soared
Obliquely through some cirrus cloud
Playing the wind inside out loud.
We arrived home that sorry autumn,
Wearing time with no top or bottom.

Nine

And so life must turn to death,
Forever ad infinitum,
Dust to dust and breath to breath,
An astronomical sum…
I ponder immortality -
Her induction to stake a claim,
Driven into humanity
Gloriously bled in her name…
Yet these lines I duly give
Will in nature fade away –
Transformed it seems we live
Eternity in a day…
       Raven's soul of love is power,
       Still as yet a wind-blown flower.

❋

Sal, Bob and Ishpa paddled north
Just to ride for what it was worth;
It felt good in their old canoe;
And to ponder the water blue

During the course of that day's trip
The heat compelled them stop and sip
The water and to reminisce,
As softly the lofty pines did hiss…
Then to the shore they took a swim,
Naked, before the sun grew dim.
Raven remained with me feeling glum;
Also, of course, Astrophel our chum,
Both of whom seemed discordant,
In the sense they were mordant,
Because Crow was vindicated
As God, then syndicated –
Metamorphed a metaphor –
A super-human guarantor
For all God-fearing people
Who prayed under a steeple,
Or any holy place
And dominion of race;
All beholden to a great lie,
Never certain never to die…
Time had run out and she was scared,
However Raven was unprepared,
Though she had not spoken a word,
In spite of her life being absurd…
At this time we knew of the plane,
Flying nearby in our terrain,

None other than our man Orley,
Who for long years had most sorely
Set out to unlock the puzzle
In spite of the police muzzle
That no one believed what he thought,
How his efforts had come to naught;
He appeared now munching nachos,
Exhibiting a mad pathos…
His plane droned on for awhile,
As we followed in sub-space guile,
When he dipped his wing for a sweep,
My worst fears reared up for this creep.
Towards our very lake headed,
He couldn't know what I dreaded
That something made him suspicious,
Perhaps a flash of auspicious
Sun reflecting off of some glass
From their cabin as he did pass…
Onto the next lake he landed,
And went ashore as demanded…
At this point Raven took her leave,
Unsure as I what to perceive,
So anticlimactic
So extragalactic –
Life defined in a moment
At some pent up foment…

In the garden looking about
Bound to her fate without a doubt…
Meanwhile Orley came to our lake
Up the creek around like a snake,
Behind the log house and clearing,
In awe at the most endearing
Garden meticulously tilled
When breaking silence a loon trilled.
There he stopped and so gazed
At Raven who stood unfazed.
Behind him the sun had almost set,
Her eyes like jewels in carcenet.
—Orley, what a momentous day!
I can see you've been led astray.
He put a hand through his pepper hair,
Feeling crushed from her surreal stare…
—I found you, he said, *I declare,*
If ever a man was more aware,
You haven't aged in twenty years,
Albeit the sum of my fears…
—I'm genetically modified,
Piped Raven, *Uncodified,*
A new word however implied,
Doesn't mean I'm not bona fide.
—Well, Jane, after all, I'm not nuts,
Yet feel the pain of a thousand cuts;

And learned to live with this complaint —
Lost in the dark a sinning saint...
—Likewise, Orley, this you may know:
I'm an alien whose blood does flow
In veins like yours with pumping heart —
A passion-play that you're a part;
You see we have a fate to vaunt,
Mine is mine but yours to haunt,
Yet I must not know the design,
Otherwise nothing to enshrine:
But for one last dance,
I would take a chance,
To put your hex
On exo sex
For the historians
And phantasmagorians,
Deemed in your sensing
Like pollen dispensing
An ecstasy to triumph over tears,
Staged to the sound of human jeers...
Orley said, *You make me nervous,*
Speaking to do some such service;
I'm not here to dissemble, Jane,
For all I know you're from Ukraine —
So where are the others,
Your sisters or brothers?

He looked on to pass,
But she showed some sass…
She moved this way and that to block his way,
When he feigned to move pretending to play.
They both stood there so very close –
She could smell his breath, a double dose –
Nachos and nerves reeked in advance,
Reveling in her this private prance –
Helpless, he was drawn to her eyes,
Those innocent orbs did mesmerize,
Crowning him king of the hermit world,
Where all of his dreams now unfurled
With compelling velocity,
And sexual ferocity;
He held her not able to resist
The force in her eyes did so persist;
She bade him on like he was dumb,
Waiting in the wings rendered numb;
Then he knew what was her pleasure,
To lay her down in token measure –
When a crow gawked in the trees,
And leaves scratched in the breeze,
Unsuspecting, his piece she lifted,
When on the ground she then shifted…
The loud shot resounded with a crack
And Raven went lifeless on her back…

My systems shuddered for many miles,
Sounding dull rippled thuds down pine aisles;
In a pain-seared gravity wave
In no way that I could behave –
All I saw was the setting sun,
Crimson magenta and the gun
In her hand and bloodless wound;
Hole in her heart black-festooned…
Orley in shock now found cover,
Looking at his would-be lover
With a halo about her head,
Fading slowly as she was dead.
He wept, *Why did you kill yourself?*
Cursing his luck and lack of stealth…
At that time the Loons had just beached,
And hearing the shot they ran and reached
The sad killing ground
Where Raven was found,
Splayed notoriously
Dead ingloriously –
Such a life now forsaken,
When Orley appeared shaken;
Sal, frenzied, ran straight at him;
Bob fired his gun as day did dim,
Sure that Orley caused Raven's death,
There with deadened eyes and no breath;

Orley panicked and shot them point blank,
Then retreated hit in his shank.
Ishpa cried to the sky and me…
All became silent and eerie…

※

The Arctic sky was grey behind
The bleak land and blustery wind,
As shrieking terns and gulls flew about
Astrophel and I were without doubt
Unable to process what was inside,
Our fusion brains so woe betide;
Our sister and brother were gone –
Our symbiosis so withdrawn…
That even after all this time,
Mortal life but a couplet rhyme.
The Loons huddled in deerskins,
Bear blanket and moccasins,
Confused and pained on top of the globe,
Caused by Orley the xenophobe,
Who as spoiler everlast,
Was in himself aghast.
Then ascending the cirrus sky,

In sorrow after our goodbye
It was time to open my screen,
And summon Raven to convene
Her purple phœnix real and clear,
Pixilated as a mirror;
With cautious step they approached
Each other to the divide encroached,
Rushing suddenly to rejoice,
Venting feelings in one voice,
Pertaining to this tragedy –
Something new – a dramedy,
In that what was calamity
Metamorphed into amity –
Here was the juxtaposition,
They could touch at the partition
With kissing lips as best able
To make most of a sad fable –
Bobby and Ishpa head to head,
Never again to take to bed…
They spoke in a quiet confidence,
Flowing tears of tragic providence,
Not to be termed at all a waste,
But a martyrdom, if in haste,
Forgiven in the eyes of nature,
A higher traffic in stature:
—*And this*, said Raven, *Is our salvation.*

Her technological consolation,
Though her fate now tarnished,
Waxed in fact rather varnished,
In that our little collective,
Albeit somewhat subjective,
Opened the shades of knowledge learned,
And sent to oblivion a monster spurned.
And so dear Raven went on,
Saying, *Now the automaton;*
My true self can be no more,
I cannot feel to the core –
My tears have filled the Pacific,
Thus was life not so terrific:
Down the ages like a germ,
I'd out-lived my use full term,
Since no one can tell,
What was simply hell,
When potion nor pardon cannot purge
Forfeited love and incessant urge –
What was innocent one day relents
To that ecstasy for all intents
A medication making right
Justification in delight,
Engendered in my juicy loins,
Sometimes sold for a few coins,
As we do derive

The will to survive –
–But why, Raven, why did you kill
The very love I yearned to fill?
–Violet, my love, in spite of tears
Unswell your cheeks open your ears,
Smile to the world, it will bemuse,
The end of my life will defuse,
What more can I say?
I did it my way –
I chose to die as I lived,
See how we're revived…
My time like Crow had come,
It was our rule of thumb;
I will always be right here,
So you have nothing to fear;
You, like our Makwa will live long,
Together you are my swan song;
You are the legacy of Panchulan,
You are one of us born as human…
They spoke as if nothing had changed,
But for the divide were estranged,
Violet smiled saying she was the sequel,
Redeemed from carnage of the prequel…
Then Johann Bach now played a piece
With his sons and Botticelli's niece –
His harpsichord led the Concerto,

With a recorder, lute and cello,
The Loons smiled and all were upraised
When Siddhartha came back unfazed,
Saying, *Kali! You have won the fight —*
The victory yours — you earned the right.
Then he greeted Yeshu, who appeared,
Being careful not to have interfered;
Both were lovers of her, who smiled,
And Yeshu seemed a bit beguiled,
Seeing Lydia his wife,
For eternal life…
Yeshu looked into her eyes of amethyst:
—Lydia, love, here we shall subsist
Likened to heaven where not a word
Has lost its way like the wayward bird —
We're out at sea on this marble blue,
Your resurrection long overdue…
So we preside doomed to observe
All the world as your hors d'oeuvre;
In our hearts there is holy fire,
And that is all that we require;
Damn the church, damn its laws —
Ecumenical flaws
That make shambles of our fame,
Nothing doing nothing the same…
Come, Lydia, my apostle Queen,

Our love that Peter deemed obscene;
He founded a church in my name
That from the start I did disclaim,
Whereby they became anti-Christ,
Co-opting love into a heist –
A political faith poised to kill
All who chose to defend my will…
Forced the exile of our child,
To the forests of Britain wild;
These stones I minister as the one,
As you're my kin and I'm the son;
Let it be known Yeshu the Jew,
Kneels not in a pagan pew…
Then kissing Lydia on the lips,
And lingered there while he slipped
His hand to her lily breast,
She said, *We, the dispossessed,*
Have been much maligned, oppressed
By evil doers – devils possessed,
Who stole from me Yeshu's bequest –
His true apostle put to the test;
Not just me but the feminine,
All the cures of our medicine –
And so they tortured, burned and killed –
Lakes of blood from innocents spilled,
All for an ideal, misinformed,

Like a plague of locusts swarmed…
Dear Yeshu, forgive our debacle,
Our human mores that we unshackle…
Sweet memory: remember Cana?
Before you wedded your Pana…
Dear Miriam, beautiful Goddess;
A love to whom I now confess —
Falling out she took the blame,
That converted from my shame;
Her virtues were of the highest order;
Lost to the ages — time's disorder…
But as wife to Yeshu the Essene,
From his rebellion she came clean,
That so anointed our great love,
Freeing our passion, freeing the dove…
Dear husband, we stood the test of time,
Did what we could in an evil clime…
To inspire love, beauty and kindness,
In all people to disdain blindness;
The force of light over dark,
Knowing both therein a spark,
That in spite of genocide —
What Roman legions applied —
In spite of civilization,
And the true realization —
Countless means to evil ends,

Where fools proclaimed evil trends:
The religious wars,
The Nazi horrors,
Its brutal thugs
With killer mugs,
Utterly cruel,
The stupid ghoul,
Stalin the Soviet,
The victims unquiet;
Untold millions —
Ghostly billions,
The ideologues,
Sick demagogues...
We're still here to light the way,
No matter what 'til judgment day;
Now that we've unlocked our souls
In the key to the Dead Sea scrolls,
To open the door to the truth,
Spikenard with a shot of vermouth...
And so I used them both,
And then swore under oath:
I would save as many as I could,
Like my old friend Robin Hood —
It drove me so crazy
Like a wind-blown daisy...
The more I tried

The more defied,
Until my time in this vortex,
Slowed to a halt my cortex,
That finally I took my life,
Simple as a two-octave fife,
A shot in the heart
After playing my part
In a martyring dance,
Like Miriam in France,
Whom I betrayed,
In fate arrayed,
To have lived through the ages,
And so turned many pages…
You see, friends, now you know me,
Though long envied how I was free,
But I think on her years in Gaul,
Away from that madman Paul,
Who ordained our marriage,
Deemed unlawful miscarriage,
Whose compliance we subverted,
Though Miriam was deserted —
Explained in Revelation
As pesher in translation.
All beneath the storied dragon,
Where blind fools hitched their wagon…
Now we must stay together,

The same birds of a feather —
Yet the curtain call ends the show,
Dust to dust no more can we know
Why we live and die,
That love does belie
My infamous flower quenching thirst
So much so that my heart just burst...
The eternal moment was
Remembered here because
Love is love and that I love you,
Heaven's a sphere whose canon true
Ascends from Precambrian rock,
Where loons call and woodpeckers knock —
Ducklings paddle and mother's squawk;
White-throated sparrows and red-tailed hawk,
Sing and soar over lakes supreme,
Where we herald the sun and dream
At the heart of the wilderness,
Whereof these spirits we address
The call of the wind and wave
Over and over to save
Generations to come on its crest,
Willful, wild and youthfully blessed,
The stuff of dreams so sublime —
The omnipotence of time,
Giving it ears and eyes, a place,

Where together we'll roam in space…

And so she stopped as tears glistened,

And Crow and Sal who had listened,

Stepped up to allay her cries,

And haunted look in amethyst eyes…

Which I alone had mine to the skies,

Having burned through history's lies…

The pines whispered our tale so told:

Now is silence in from the cold;

Now it's written and this tale ends,

Bidden from whence the west wind wends.

Epilogue

On earth these few thousand years –
The blue ball of my heart and fears –
My twin of sorts, Raven, must rest
With those interred she loved best.
In her time she had learned the game,
Having shunned unparalleled fame,
Although at times not glamorous,
Still ambrosial, amorous –
In nature we need not ask why –
Heedless is but a purple sky,
That subsumed in a holy grail,
A living goddess did prevail;
So in this meter used by bards,
Give Aphrodite my regards,
And I, Zephyrus, feeling bled,
Torn inside-out heavy as lead,
Must now depart for a new dream –
I see the sun alight its seam –
If technical, and somewhat odd,
Casting down the veil of god,
We beg your favor a higher grace,
Given nature and our human race.

The End.